# K9 INVESTIGATION ERRORS

## Other titles in the
## *K9 Professional Training Series*

## Other K9 titles from Brush Education

# K9 INVESTIGATION ERRORS

## A Manual for Avoiding Mistakes

Dr. Resi Gerritsen
Ruud Haak

*K9 PROFESSIONAL TRAINING SERIES*

*DOG TRAINING PRESS*
*AN IMPRINT OF*

16 17 18 19 20  5 4 3 2 1

Printed and manufactured in Canada

Brush Education Inc.
www.brusheducation.ca
contact@brusheducation.ca

Editorial: Meaghan Craven
Cover Design: John Luckhurst; cover image: iStock/Photo by Yuri Arcurs
Interior Design: Carol Dragich, Dragich Design

Based on *K9 Fraud!* also by Dr. Resi Gerritsen and Ruud Haak. Updated content and a new chapter.

**Library and Archives Canada Cataloguing in Publication**
Gerritsen, Resi, author
K9 investigation errors : a manual for avoiding mistakes / Dr. Resi Gerritsen, Ruud Haak.

(K9 professional training series)

Includes bibliographical references.
Issued in print and electronic formats.
ISBN 978-1-55059-672-4 (paperback).—ISBN 978-1-55059-673-1 (pdf).—
ISBN 978-1-55059-674-8 (mobi).—ISBN 978-1-55059-675-5 (epub)

1. Working dogs—Training—Handbooks, manuals, etc.   2. Working dogs—Sense organs—Handbooks, manuals, etc.   3. Odors—Handbooks, manuals, etc.   4. Criminal investigation—Handbooks, manuals, etc.   I. Haak, Ruud, author   II. Title.   III. Series: K9 professional training series

SF428.2.G473 2016        636.7'0886        C2016-901958-6
                                            C2016-901959-4

# Contents

# Disclaimer

While the contents of this book are based on substantial experience and expertise, working with dogs involves inherent risks, especially in dangerous settings and situations. Anyone using approaches described in this book does so entirely at their own risk, and both the author and publisher disclaim any liability for any injuries or other damage that may be sustained.

# Introduction

During the course of an investigation, search-dog handlers have been known to make mistakes. Sometimes these are honest errors in judgement or the result of poor training—poorly trained handlers and/or dogs—but sometimes handlers deliberately perpetrate errors. Some of the most important reasons for investigation errors include the handler's:

1. lack of knowledge about influencing dogs,
2. lack of dog-training skills,
3. desire to hide the dog's poor quality or characteristics,
4. need to solve a case quickly,
5. interest in benefiting financially from a specific result, and
6. aspiration to appear to be a better dog handler than others.

In this book we will consider at length errors and fraudulent practices committed by search-dog handlers. We will present and discuss a variety of cases and causes of errors carried out during the course of scent-identification lineups, tracking, and mantrailing. Since there is no international standard for scent-identification lineups, we've included a chapter with recommendations for just such a standard. These recommendations are based on the scientifically established Dutch standard for scent-identification lineups.

We also describe the training for this method in detail. Since the beginning of the use of dogs for scent-identification lineups, tracking, and mantrailing, mistakes—both unintended and intentional—have detracted from the reputation of dogs and handlers in investigative work. In particular, handlers have often been guilty of influencing their dogs. To stress the significance of this problem, we extensively discuss the conscious and unconscious influencing of the dog by its handler or by helpers, also called the Clever Hans Effect.

Undetected errors in dog handling procedures lead to miscarriages of justice, including prosecution and incarceration (even death) of innocents, and they are absolutely unforgivable. So we also include a chapter devoted to how dog handlers (and their supervisors) can avoid making such errors—deliberate or not—with all kinds of search dogs.

*Dr. Resi Gerritsen and Ruud Haak*

# Scent-Identification Lineups

"Thousands of Dutch police scent identification tests void," read the headlines of newspapers across the Netherlands in 2006. "All scent identification lineups which took place from 1997 to 2006 by police dogs in the district North and East Netherlands may not be used anymore as evidence in criminal trials," the Board of Attorney General wrote in a letter to the public prosecutors.[1]

In October 2006, two police-dog handlers from the North and East Netherlands police unit admitted to the court of justice in the Dutch town of Leeuwarden that they did not always perform scent-identification lineups according to the rules. In several lineups, the police-dog handlers said, the dog handler already knew where the suspect's odor was located in the lineup. After this admission, the court immediately acquitted the suspects concerned, and the National Department of Criminal Investigation investigated each member of the district's team of seven police-dog handlers, who were immediately removed from their positions.

Since April 2011, the Prosecutor's Office in the Netherlands has not permitted the results of scent-identification tests as evidence in lawsuits. In a number of lawsuits, dog handlers have admitted that they made mistakes, prompting almost one hundred convicts to request a review of judgments. The dogs have been given other duties.

## Early Protocols and Success

Police forces in Europe have used scent-identification lineups since the beginning of the 20th century. In these lineups, trained police dogs compare human scent found on objects at crime scenes (the *corpus delicti*) with the odor of a suspect. As early as 1910, Dr. Friedo Schmidt from Stralsund, Germany, recognized the importance of properly saving and storing *corpus delicti*:

> By no means should the article be left at the scene or be taken in hand by the criminal investigator. This must be common knowledge to every man working at the crime scene. The article may also not be wrapped in paper or packed in a wooden or cardboard box because before long it will take the odor of the other material. I suggest glass containers as the best means of storage. Glass is an inert material. Substances such as sweat and blood incur no changes in contact with glass. Every separate article, as much as size allows, must be put in an appropriately sized, wide-necked, sealable, glass receptacle equipped with a glass-stopper. Such containers have the advantage of transparency, so that the article, such as a handkerchief, can easily pass from hand to hand and important details, such as a monogram, can also be observed whilst in the receptacle.[2]

### THE DUWE MURDER CASE

A key historic figure in the history of suspect identification by dogs is Inspector Bussenius from Braunschweig, Germany. Bussenius was a champion of police-dog work and a very good police-dog trainer, too. His work in Braunschweig provided authorities with evidence that police dogs could do what police people cannot—and that their actions are indeed valuable. In particular, Bussenius's success with his German shepherd Harras von der Polizei in the Duwe murder case at Hagenhof (near Braunschweig) in June 1903 gave the world the first proof of a trained dog's value in the investigation of homicide cases. Harras von der Polizei's success in the Duwe case is often seen as a turning point in the history of the police dog.

Dr. Friedo Schmidt wrote about this case in 1911:

An 11-year-old girl was killed at the Hagenhof farm in the German village of Königslutter near Braunschweig on June 3, 1903. The forensic research team did not come up with results, although one of the farmhands was suspected. After days of continuous but fruitless investigation, the public prosecutor asked Inspector Bussenius from Braunschweig to try to find the murderer with his German shepherd dog Harras von der Polizei. After their arrival at the Hagenhof farm—four days after the homicide—all 12 employees of the farm were placed in a line in the yard. After that Harras was brought to the crime scene, where Inspector Bussenius commanded him to sniff the bloodstains and the surrounding area of the crime scene. The dog immediately picked up a track. First he briefly scanned one of the forensic investigators who had visited the crime scene earlier. Before long, the dog left him and continued tracking. The dog then sniffed each person standing in the line, one after the other. When he reached the eighth position in line, Harras suddenly hurled himself at the man, who cried out loudly in protest. The accused man was the suspected farmhand Duwe. The test was repeated two times. Each time, the people in the line changed positions, but the result was always the same: Harras hurling himself furiously at Duwe and not paying attention to the other people. After that, Duwe was arrested. In the beginning Duwe tried to deny the murder, but soon he made a full confession. Duwe was condemned to death.[3]

## Early Dutch Scent Identifications

The first Dutch scent identifications started in about 1914. Officer Jacob Water of the Amsterdam police and his dog Albert, a long-haired Belgian shepherd, traveled throughout the Netherlands to follow tracks and identify suspects. The work the pair did was impressive, and principles arising from Albert and Water's efforts became the foundation for developments in Dutch scent-identification lineups and general search work done by police dogs.

## MURDER IN THE MILK FACTORY

One case Water and Albert investigated involved of the director of a milk factory whose throat was cut with a razor. A hat and a razor were found in the factory, near the spot where the man was killed. Water wrote about this case in his memoirs:

> When first asked for assistance, Albert was given odor from the razor and later on from the hat. He tracked through the factory then outside to a tree where the murderer had probably mounted a bicycle and left the scene. In the meantime, it was rumored that a man known to the police had been seen in the vicinity. Almost three weeks later, this man was arrested. However, he denied being the murderer. Again Albert was asked for help. The suspect was placed in a circle together with other people. After sniffing at the razor, the dog pointed out the suspect without hesitation, even though the man continued to deny involvement with the murder. Then a second test was carried out. The hats of all those present were spread out on the ground along with the hat found near the crime scene. Albert sniffed at the suspect and then went to the collection of hats. Soon he picked out a hat, but not the one found near the crime scene. After searching again, Albert brought the hat found at the crime scene to his handler. The first hat belonged to the suspect: he had been wearing it when he was arrested.[4]

Officer Water concluded that this hat was picked out by the dog first because it contained the strongest odor of the suspect.

**Figure 1.1** Albert, the long-haired Belgian shepherd belonging to Officer Jacob Water of the Amsterdam police in 1914.

Hallo!... Geïllustreerd Weekblad. 7

## Roofmoord op een fabrieksdirecteur te St. Oedenrode

**Figure 1.2** Albert performs a scent-identification lineup on hats in the case of a murdered director of a milk factory. Top left: The arrest. Right: Mr. Van Ledden Hulsebosch giving Albert scent from the found razor.

## TESTING ALBERT

Prof. Dr. F.J.J. Buytendijk, an expert in animal behavior, decided to test Albert's scenting ability. Six people were lined up. Each person took a pebble into his hand, and at a signal they all threw their pebbles onto a path strewn with pebbles. Albert was allowed to sniff the hands of one of the individuals, and Officer Water then commanded the dog to search. Albert searched the path, sniffing intently at each of the pebbles thrown onto the path, until he reached the "correct" pebble and retrieved it. Buytendijk wrote about this incident his book:

> It was interesting to observe how the dog's behavior changed the moment he discovered the "correct" pebble. While quietly searching from one spot to the other, all at once his ears stood on end, and with fast movements of nose and mouth, he isolated the pebble from the area, then quickly retrieved it. The dog behaved in a totally different manner when he, either through the influence of his handler or other distractions, picked up a wrong pebble. In these cases, the dog reacted in an uncertain, almost shy manner.[5]

## THE BEESD MURDER CASE

Another case involving Officer Water and Albert was the murder of the mayor of the Dutch town of Beesd. In the last year of World War I, a burglary took place in Beesd's town hall; the perpetrators' intention was to steal ration cards. A ladder was placed at the back of the building to reach a window on the first floor, which was opened with a crowbar. The mayor, who was probably woken up by the noise, went into the town clerk's office to investigate and was shot dead. Officer Water wrote:

> At the crime scene, Albert found the pistol and crowbar. Three men loitering in the vicinity of Beesd were arrested for vagrancy and placed in a big circle among other people. Confronted with the scent on the crowbar, Albert pointed out one of the suspects by barking at him. Of course the suspect denied it, but he was taken away by a gendarme. Again Albert took the odor from the crowbar and, sniffing, he went back among the men gathered in the circle. He stopped in front of a hunchback who, after being shown the pistol and the crowbar, conceded that the crowbar belonged to the person who had first been picked out by the dog in the circle. "And the pistol?" he was asked. "The pistol belongs to Mr. De Rijk, who left in the direction of the Belgian border," the man answered. Immediately a warrant for his arrest was issued to all

border crossings. "But what did you do?" the hunchback was asked. "Well," he said, "I laid a plank over a ditch and placed the ladder against the town hall." And when questioned about whether the first man, the owner of the crowbar, had had anything to do with the affair, he answered: "Yes, Sir. He forced the window open for Mr. De Rijk."[6]

And as a result of this testimony, the case was closed.

## Discriminating Similar Odors

In around 1918, scent identification in the Netherlands was led by the forensic expert Dr. C.J. van Ledden Hulsebosch from Amsterdam. He describes several cases in a book he wrote about his 40 years as a police investigator. Some of the cases, such as "the murderer with manure," illustrate the precise manner in which Van Ledden Hulsebosch worked.

### THE MURDERER WITH MANURE

In January 1918, Officer Water, his dog Albert, and Bob, Amsterdam's first police dog, had to solve a murder case through scent identification. Although this case is not an example of dogs working with human scent, it does illustrate the dog's ability to clearly discriminate between similar odors. Officer Water depicted the situation as follows in his memoir:

> Near the town of Breezand, a farmer was found dead. Based on fingerprints and other clues, two people were arrested for the murder. One of the suspect's fingerprints were found at the crime scene, and this person confessed. In his confession, he related how he and the other man had pulled off their shoes and then climbed through a small window in order to gain entry to the barn. Dropping through the window, they landed in a cowshed, where the second suspect slipped, his right foot ending up in the manure gutter. With his hand, he wiped most of the manure off his sock. He then stepped back into his shoe wearing the soiled sock.

Knowing this, Mr. Van Ledden Hulsebosch wanted to examine these shoes. A gendarme went to the suspect's cell to fetch them. But the suspect smelled a rat and told the gendarme he had visited the cattle market in the town of Purmerend that Tuesday, and he had gotten cow manure on his sock there. To our noses, the manure of one cow smells much the same as the other, so the dung would not necessarily be incriminating. But Van Ledden Hulsebosch thought dogs could tell the difference between manure from different cowsheds. So he asked the gendarme from Breezand to bring him cow manure from 12 different cowsheds—including from where the murder had taken place—in 12 clean jam jars. The jam jars were numbered and a list of the owners of the cowsheds was compiled. Now Van Ledden Hulsebosch took 72 equal pieces of paper and divided them into six series, each numbered from one to 12, according to the numbers on the jam jars. Manure was spread on the numbered papers, and then these were distributed throughout the courtyard of the police headquarters, between shrubs and in all sorts of places.

After this was done, a special experiment began. Mr. Van Ledden Hulsebosch first wanted to test whether the dogs were able to find dung from a particular shed by means of "sorting." To do this, I [Officer Water] took a piece of paper with manure on it, let the dogs smell it, and commanded them to "search." Immediately the dogs started searching around and soon they found all the papers with the same number. To guard against coincidence, the test was repeated several times with other manure papers, all with the same result. As this experiment proved that the dogs could indeed discriminate between the manure from the different cowsheds, they were presented the left shoe to take scent. The dogs hesitated and stood still. Apparently they did not recognize the scent, and they sniffed around listlessly. Then they were presented the right shoe, which as mentioned before had been stained with manure. Immediately their manner changed. They started wagging their tails and started searching. Very soon all the pieces of paper with the number of the jam jar containing the manure out of the cowshed where the murder had taken place

**Figure 1.3** Example of an investigation error from the year 1919: At a crime scene, Mr. Van Ledden Hulsebosch discovered numerous fingerprints. However, he forgot to take the "fingers" (the police term for fingerprints) of the victim. He sent a message to the village constable, asking him to send along the victim's "fingers." The constable took this request literally, cut off the victim's fingers, and sent them in a glass jar to Amsterdam!

were laid out before me [Officer Water]. And as if he had wanted a crowning glory on his work, Albert brought me the whole jam jar a few seconds later.[7]

## Protecting the Evidence

A 1930 report by the Amsterdam police describes a special box that was made for the purposes of scent-identification lineups:

> Since the objects have to be kept strictly separated and also have to be transported, we designed a "sorting box" that has proved to be excellent in practice. We built the box in two forms: one to hang on the frame of a bicycle, and one to place on the luggage carrier. The first-mentioned model is divided into 6 parts that each can contain 10 to 15 objects. The cover can be mounted with thumb nuts (see B in Figure 1.4). When the mixing of odors has to be prevented, rubber strips (c) are mounted on the sides of the partition. By turning the thumb nuts, these strips are pressed and so form an airtight partition. At (a) you see forceps, used to pick up objects. The sorting box for the luggage carrier (Figure 1.5) was made in the same way and has also been very helpful. With these boxes, material for several dogs can be transported and also kept for some time. After using the boxes, it is necessary to ventilate them well and so we have two boxes—one to use, and one to ventilate.[8]

**Figure 1.4** The sorting box lodged on the frame of a bicycle belonging to the Amsterdam police. (1930)

**Figure 1.5** The sorting box placed on the luggage carrier of an officer's bike. (1930)

## Problems in Early Lineup Protocols

The manner in which scent-identifications lineups in the Netherlands were to be conducted in forensic practice changed over the years in accordance with scientific developments. The current standard operational protocol is the result of history, experience, and scientific research.

In the 1920s and 1930s, the scent-identification lineup consisted of a lineup of people. The object that contained the scent of the perpetrator, the *corpus delicti*, was kept in a preserving jar. The suspect was made to stand in a row or circle with several other people referred to as "foils." The dog handler would let his dog smell the *corpus delicti*, and the dog would then compare the scent with that of the people in the lineup. The dog would indicate a match by barking at the person. The lineup usually consisted of six people, and the dog had to repeat his choice two or three times. The handler knew beforehand who the suspect was.

An obvious drawback to this version of the human lineup is that the subject, simply by being frightened of being considered a suspect, could react in a way that influences the dog's choice. The dog could choose someone based on this behavior rather than because of the scent.

**Figure 1.6** A scent-identification lineup of worn shoes, circa 1950.

In later years, the people in the lineup were replaced by objects. Several people were asked to put something that belonged to them in a row on the ground. An object that belonged to the suspect was included in the row. Whether each of the objects in the row belonged to a different person or if some belonged to the same person is a part of the procedure that is lost to history. But we do know that the *corpus delicti* was kept in the preserving jar. The handler would let his dog smell the *corpus delicti*, and the dog would then investigate the lineup of objects and retrieve the object with the matching human scent. If this object belonged to the suspect, it would be replaced in another position in the row and the dog would be asked to repeat his choice a second or third time. Again, the handler always knew which object belonged to the suspect.

In 1932 Professor Buytendijk issued a clear warning regarding the foreknowledge the police-dog handler had about suspects when carrying out a scent lineup:

> First of all, it is necessary that all tests are performed in such a way that inadvertent influencing of the dog by the handler is excluded. Second, it is recommended that dogs choose between similar objects. Once I saw a scent-identification test that obviously succeeded, but it was absolutely incorrectly performed. May the following report be a warning to help ensure the objective use of the police dog:
>
> In the house of detention was a suspect and the investigators wanted to know if coat "A," found at the crime scene, belonged to him. In the courtyard, six coats were lined up, one of which was coat "A," and the five others belonging to officers. After the police dog had been allowed to take the scent of the suspect, he retrieved coat "A." Such a test doesn't prove anything. Coat "A," of course, would have a totally different odor profile than the coats belonging to the officers. Imagine that the odors were visible. In this case, the dog would see five gray coats and a single red one, so there would be a good chance that the dog would retrieve the one that was different from the others, since it stood out. Only if all objects belong to the same

**Figure 1.7** To prevent direct contact with the dog in the human lineup system (top), people were made to stand behind a screen. (Rotterdam Police, circa 1970)

group of odor, and are optically identical in measurement and form, can there be a chance of obtaining reliable results. Even more dangerous is to let a dog choose a person from a lineup of men based on the odor of an object, even when the handler doesn't know the test or suspects someone, because there always will be a good chance that the dog would react to the slightest movement of one of the men in line.[9]

In later variants of the human lineup system, people were made to stand behind a screen to prevent direct contact with the dog. Later, police would place fans behind the lineup to blow the scent of each person straight through the screen.

**Figure 1.8** Transport of handler and police search dog, early 1960s.

## Problems with the Objects

Even after the human lineup was replaced by a row of objects, problems still occurred. It became obvious that dogs preferred retrieving certain types of objects over others and that the lineup was, therefore, not very objective. So in the 1950s, the police started to ensure that the lineup consisted of similar objects. Bunches of keys were chosen as standard objects since the police dogs had ample experience with them as training objects. Now uniform bunches of keys were cleaned in boiling water and handed out to several people, including the suspect, to hold in their pockets or hands. These keys were then placed in paper envelopes or preserving bottles until the scent-identification lineup took place. At this point, the dog was given the scent of the *corpus delicti* and had to retrieve the matching bunch of keys several times. Each time, before the dog went back to the lineup, the retrieved keys were repositioned in the row of objects.

Further changes to scent-lineup procedures in the Netherlands were made during the 1960s. The *corpus delicti* came to be preserved in modern plastic containers, and bunches of keys were replaced with aluminum tubes, usually engraved with a number. But the aluminum tubes proved to be too soft and were easily damaged by the dogs' teeth, so they were replaced again by stainless steel tubes (which are still in use).

In 1960s Rotterdam, police used a standard method to obtain the scent of both the suspect and the foils. First, three people held two tubes each in their pockets; these tubes served as foils in the row. The suspect was asked to hold three or four tubes. If a suspect was unwilling to hold the tubes in his or her hand, the tubes would be placed in the armpits of his or her jacket in order to pick up scent. The row was composed of six or seven tubes from which the dog could choose after smelling the *corpus delicti*. The dog had to investigate the row several times over, and a fresh tube with the suspect's scent was used each time; the same foil tubes were used over and over again. The handler usually knew the position of the suspect's tube, but several preferred not to know to avoid inadvertently signaling its location to the dog.

## Correcting the Dog during Lineups

In 1968, a scent-identification lineup played an important role in a court case concerning the murder of a pub owner in the Dutch village of Oirschot. The suspect was a tramp. The tramp and several other people scented several tubes by holding them in their hands. These tubes were duly put into a lineup. The dog handler who conducted the lineup knew which of the tubes had been scented by the tramp. When he saw that his dog intended to retrieve a tube that was scented by one of the foils, he corrected his dog verbally with a little "Fie." The dog continued to search and next retrieved the tube that had been scented by the tramp.

The controversial process was actively discussed in court. All of the evidence, including that collected at the scent-identification lineup, was examined critically and the suspect was acquitted twice. An important part of the discussion concerned the dog handler's prior knowledge of the position of the tube scented by the tramp. Although most people agreed that it would have been better if this were not the case, they did not seem fully aware of the consequences of a handler knowing. Even if the handler does not give a verbal cue to steer the dog clear of a particular object, we know that dogs do react to signals that handlers are themselves unaware of. A slight catching of the breath or a relaxation of muscles when the dog is paying attention to the "correct" tube can be involuntary, unconscious. If a handler unconsciously reacts this way over and over again, the dog will pick up on it as a reliable cue that leads to being rewarded for a job well done.

## The 1980s Fitting-Room Murder

In the 1980s, the scent-identification lineup again came under fire in the Dutch courts related to a famous case, the Paskamermoord (Fitting-Room Murder). On Friday, November 30, 1984, in Zaanstad (a town close to Amsterdam) at about 11:30 a.m., a customer in the dress boutique Manouk found the body of 20-year-old shop assistant Sandra van Raalten in a fitting room. It was a particularly bloody murder: the girl had been gagged with a handkerchief, bound hand and foot with strips from the fitting-room curtain, and her throat had been cut. She lay in a big puddle of blood; blood was found 12 feet (1.5 m) up the walls of the fitting room. Although about 250 Dutch guilders in the cash register was missing, and so was Van Raalten's gold jewelry, the police did not believe robbery was the chief concern of the perpetrator, arguing that during a robbery, an attacker would not take great pains to gag and bind the victim. The murderer's motive remained unclear. In the autopsy, no signs of sexual contact were found, and forensics found no signs of the perpetrator in the boutique.

The brutal murder attracted attention in the press, and the police brought about 30 men into action to investigate, but they did not make progress. The investigation did not lead to results, just a lot of loose ends and people contradicting each other. Two years later, another team of investigators took over the case, and suspicion led them to a friend of Sandra, 33-year-old local bicycle dealer Rob van Zaane. In 1986, two years after the murder, two scent-identification lineups were performed with Van Zaane as the suspect. In one lineup, the handkerchief was used, and ten days later the strip of curtain used to tie the girl's ankles was used. The same police dog, Tim, was on duty for both lineups, and in both lineups, Van Zaane was pointed out. In the first trial, Van Zaane was convicted and sentenced to 12 years in prison based largely on this evidence. During the trial, Van Zaane said it was possible he had given the handkerchief to the girl the evening before, but given an earlier statement that he never had a handkerchief with him, this testimony was not considered credible.

**Figure 1.9** Police dog Tim works out a scent-identification lineup in the mid-1980s. At that time, lineups were carried out on a rubber mat in a hall or outdoors in a police courtyard. (Police Zaanstad, 1985)

### THREE PROBLEMS WITH THE LINEUP
In appeal, another lawyer took over, and the scent-identification lineup was examined critically. Several experts were called in. Three major points were made.

*First,* the quality of the dog used for the lineups was discussed. Tim was also a trained narcotics dog, so the lawyer argued he might have approached Van Zaane due to the smell of marijuana (Van Zaane was a known drug user). It is always best to employ single-purpose dogs to avoid such a possibility.

*Second,* the quality of the objects used for the lineups was discussed. Both the handkerchief and the strip of curtain were contaminated with blood and possibly corpse odor, they had not been preserved properly, and they may have been "too old," as the lineups were conducted almost two years after the crime had been committed.

*Third,* the handler knew the position of the tube Van Zaane had scented for the purposes of the lineups.

The appeal case was dramatic: the scent-identification lineup was disqualified, the police investigators were accused of being biased against Van Zaane, and several other loose ends in the investigation became apparent. Van Zaane was acquitted, but the police and members of the public prosecution remained convinced of his guilt.

In 2001, the murder was finally solved. Improved DNA-matching techniques made it possible to match DNA found at the crime scene to a man who, at the time of the murder, had been regarded as a possible suspect. He had been interrogated during the investigation, but the police let him go due to lack of evidence. This man, a drug addict and notorious thief, died in a hospital in 1992. Van Zaane at last felt the relief of being fully cleared of suspicion.

## The 1997 Dutch Protocol
As a consequence of all the problems with lineups in the past, and after a critical, scientific review of the process by Dr. Adee Schoon

**Figure 1.10** The scent-identification room with two platforms, upon each a row of seven stainless steel scent carriers. (KLPD, 2002)

of the University of Leiden, in 1997 a new protocol for scent-identification lineups in the Netherlands was introduced. This protocol is still in use today. Detailed instructions for how to train a dog in this method are provided in Chapter 2.

According to the new protocol, a police officer is designated a "certified helper" and is tasked with preparing the lineup in a special room, where he or she places the stainless steel tubes (the scent carriers) in two rows on two platforms. The dog handler and dog are absent during the preparation of the lineup. The handler does not know the position of the different scents and, just like the helper, he or she testifies to this in the *proces verbaal* (the official report written under oath of office).

According to the protocol, the suspect's odor is one of seven different odors in the lineup. Each of the seven odors is present in each of the two rows, but in a different sequence. Five of the odors in both rows are from foils. The seventh odor belongs to a control person. The position of the odors is random due to a strict process for selection (see page 47).

Before the unleashed dog is allowed to compare the odor of the *corpus delicti* with the odors in the lineup, the dog's ability to perform is tested by asking him to search for the scent of the control person in both rows of the lineup. By doing this, the dog shows that he has no preference for or special interest in the suspect's odor. Only after positively identifying the control person in both rows may the dog compare the odor of the *corpus delicti* with the remaining six odors in each row. If the dog only responds to the suspect's odor and ignores all the other odors, his behavior is considered a "positive identification."

### THE IMPORTANCE OF THE HELPER

Clearly, if the dog handler knows the position of the suspect's odor in a lineup, the dog's investigation of the odors will not be objective. Consciously or unconsciously, the handler may somehow indicate which tube is the "right" one. Objectivity is necessary, so the certified helper's work, secretly creating the lineup of scented tubes, is key to proper procedure. The helper usually prepares the lineup by clamping the scented stainless steel tubes onto a platform. The tubes are presented according to one of 36 random sequences.

During the scent lineup, the handler must signal the helper, who is in another room and observes through a window, when the dog indicates that he has found a tube whose odor matches that of the *corpus delicti*. How the dog signals his find can vary, depending on the dog's training. Each dog's signal is annotated on his certificate; indications include barking, biting, scratching, sitting, lying down, etcetera. After an indication of a match, the dog is given a fixed reward, the details of which are also annotated on his certificate. The most common reward has the helper releasing the stainless steel tube with the matching odor from the platform so the dog can retrieve it.

**Figure 1.11** Letting the dog smell the odor of the perpetrator on an object (the *corpus delicti*). (KLPD, 2002)

## The Deventer Murder Case

The 1999 murder of Jacqueline Wittenberg, an elderly, wealthy widow from Deventer, was initially solved with the help of a scent-identification lineup. Investigators knew the murderer was someone the victim knew because she never admitted people she did not know into her house. Even people she knew she only admitted if they let her know they were coming beforehand. So when she was found murdered, but no signs of breaking and entering were found, the group of suspects was immediately limited.

The most obvious suspect was a tax specialist, Ernest Louwes, the executer of her will. He was president of the foundation that received her money, the bank account of this foundation was in his name, and he had already spent her money for private reasons, contrary to her wishes. He had a key to her house and was a regular guest. No murder weapon was found in her house. A knife was discovered two days later, under a neighbor's porch. It was moved indoors by someone who covered his hand with his sleeve. No blood was found on the knife. Later, a scent-identification lineup was executed with this knife, and the police dog pointed out the suspect. This identification was performed according to the new 1997 regulations: first, two control trials established the dog's capacity to work and ruled out potential attractiveness of the suspect's odor, and second, two trials were performed in which the dog matched the odor on the knife to the odor of the suspect.

The suspect admitted to having visited the woman on the morning of her death, but he denied a later visit and the murder. However, telephone records showed a call had been made from his mobile phone to her house shortly before the murder, a call lasting 16 seconds. This fitted into the pattern of visitors calling just before arriving, as was customary with the victim. Mobile telephones use telecom antennae distributed all over the country to connect to the telephone network. Telephone records also show which antenna is used for each call: always the one nearest to the caller. In this case, the call went through the telecom antennae in Deventer, the town the lady lived in. Again, this fitted into the pattern of calling just before arriving. The suspect admitted to the call, but he denied having been in the neighborhood. He said he was some 15 miles (25 km) away from her town. A telecom expert testified that had the call been made from the place the suspect said he'd been, it would never have gone through the antenna it did. The suspect could not have been where he said he was when he made the call. And yet, the suspect continued to deny everything.

In the lower court, he was acquitted due to lack of sufficient evidence. In the appeal in 2000, court experts testified in detail about mobile telephones and scent-identification lineups, and he was convicted and sentenced to 12 years in prison for the crime based on the combined evidence of his motive, the telephone call, and the positive scent identification. However, two years later, in 2002, the Supreme Court of the Netherlands concluded that "the knife used in the scent-identification lineup could not be the murder weapon."[10] New DNA tests showed that there were no traces of the victim or the suspect on the knife.

## PERJURY AND FORGERY

In the beginning of this chapter, we mention a letter written by the Board of Attorney General in the Netherlands from November 2006, saying that "no results of the scent-identification lineups in the period from September 1997 until March 2006 performed by police dogs in the district North and East Netherlands may be used as evidence in criminal trials." The Deventer case was one of these trials.

The seven police-dog handlers in Leeuwarden (part of the North and East Netherlands team) were prosecuted for perjury and forgery because they hadn't always performed the scent-identification lineups in accordance with the Dutch 1997 regulations. According to the rules, the dog handler cannot know the position of the scent carriers to avoid influencing the dog. Unfortunately, this was not always the case with this dog team, although on the *proces verbaal*, the officers certified under oath of office that they had complied with the regulations. In November 2007, the seven police-dog handlers were sentenced to 240 hours of penal labor. Six of the seven handlers also were deprived of office for two years. Only the dog handler who spoke up about the protocol problems and thus began the investigation was allowed to continue his work, although not in scent-identification lineups.

## "Junk Science" in the United States

Although the North and East Netherlands team did much to discredit scent lineups in the Netherlands between 1997 and 2006, the Dutch protocol, when followed to the letter, is an excellent process. The United States, on the other hand, still has no standards or procedures in place for scent-identification lineups. On his or her own, each dog handler is authorized to create a lineup in the way he or she thinks best, and there are no officially certified helpers, handlers, or even dogs. This is a bad situation that leads to a lot of mistakes, and even fraud.

In October 2009, Ed Lavandera of CNN reported on the Innocence Project of Texas's critique of scent lineups, which called the practice of scent-identification lineups a forensic tool "junk science that's being used by prosecutors and judges to convict people."[11] The Innocence Project, a nonprofit group dedicated to discovering and overturning wrongful convictions, wants state governments to ban the use of scent-identification lineups. It says an unknown number of people have been wrongly accused or convicted because of the lineups. We will discuss some of these cases in the following chapters.

In the United States, the most common technique is as follows. First, police investigators obtain human scent from a suspect and the odor of foils by rubbing gauze pads on their bodies or clothes. These gauze pads are then placed in tin cans. Most of the time, six numbered tins are used, and they are placed in a row outside, with three to four yards (2.7–3.7 m) between each tin. The handler gives the dog the scent of the *corpus delicti*, which is packed in a plastic bag, and then the handler and dog (kept on leash) walk down the line of tin cans. If the dog matches the scent, the dog will give a "sign," usually by stopping at the can or barking. After that, the tin can is placed in another sequence, and again handler and dog walk along the line.

### MANY FAULTS

Besides all the opportunities for fraud that exist in such a procedure, there are 10 other main problems.

1. In this lineup procedure, there is no control test that allows a handler to ascertain the dog's general working ability. A dog

can perform poorly for several reasons, usually physical or motivational. Checking the dog's ability to perform immediately before the lineup allows handlers to exclude dogs that are not performing well, which in turn increases the reliability of the outcome of the lineup.

2. This lineup process also has no procedure to allow a handler to ascertain the attractiveness of the suspect's odor to the dog. In most European procedures, attractiveness of odor is usually checked by letting the suspect be a foil in the control test. The dog has to successfully smell and then ignore the suspect's odor.

3. In a lot of non-European lineup procedures, *corpus delicti,* suspect, and foil scent traces are not collected and stored in the best way. The best way to collect and preserve scents is to use a pair of well-cleaned tongs to pick up the *corpus delicti* and scented gauze strips, and then place the items into individual, clean glass jars with twist-off lids. Then, each jar should be carefully registered, stored, and transported.

4. All procedures should ensure that the scent of the foils resembles that of the suspect. All foils should be the same sex, race, and age, and their odor should be collected at the same time.

5. Also important is that tins or jars used in lineups are cleaned out well before each use in order to avoid contamination of odors. Tins and jars should be either sterilized in a stove or washed with non-perfumed soap in a dishwasher before being boiled in clean water.

6. Sometimes police officers place the bagged, scented gauze strips into the tins or jars with their bare hands. The *corpus delicti* is also handled in this way. Again, this procedure can cause contamination of odors that may confuse the dog, thus affecting his work.

7. By placing the tins in a lineup outdoors, other odors, such as that of urine or food, can distract the dog.

8. Because the lineup is outside, the wind can mix up the odors the dog needs to investigate.

9. Because the handler keeps the dog on leash and walks with him along the lineup, the handler can unintentionally influence his or her dog by movements (walking slower or stopping, for example), voice, or tightening or loosening the leash. Handlers using dogs in scent-identification lineups must be aware of the influence they can exert with body language. The best way is always to work off leash, letting the dog smell the tins by himself. While the dog is working, the handler should be trying to keep still and not influence the dog in any way.

10. Finally, the end results of the lineup are always dubious if, after the dog correctly matches the scents, another lineup is made by placing the samples in another sequence using bare hands. This, of course, contaminates all the odors.

## LACK OF CERTIFICATION

Critics of scent-identification lineups in the United States correctly note that dog handlers are not certified or regulated, and there is not a system in place to check a dog's track record. Again, we quote Ed Lavandera of CNN: "Steve Nicely is a professional dog trainer in Austin, Texas. He's trained police dogs for 30 years and is also an expert witness. Nicely argues that there needs to be a system in place that tracks a dog's accuracy rate. 'There are no national standards,' Nicely said. 'Our standards are so lacking, it's pathetic. We should be ashamed of ourselves.'"[12]

The Innocence Project of Texas concurs:

Today, police and prosecutors are using yet another kind of junk science to win cases. This "science" involves dog handlers who testify that a dog "told" them who was present at a crime scene or whose scent was on a piece of evidence by making signals to the handler during a "scent lineup." The use of this "dog whispering" has become more and more common. Prosecutors have touted the "evidence" gained from this practice as being "as powerful as DNA evidence to support a conviction." We decided to investigate the use of this technique by Texas officials.... [We conclude:] The "science" of scent lineups in Texas has no rules, procedures or performance standards. It is being practiced by "experts" without expertise according to no rules except their own.[13]

## Scent Indentification in Criminal Cases

Scent-identification lineups are used for investigating criminal cases all over the world. Although the basic principle is always the same (matching the found odor of the perpetrator to the odor of a suspect), the material used to present the odors and the protocol followed in the lineup differs among countries. This is the result of history: the dog handlers involved in developing the lineups have typically been isolated in their different countries, and so differences have naturally evolved. Currently, however, information about the process is being shared. For example, the end of the Iron Curtain dividing Western and Eastern Europe, and the closer integration of the European countries in the European Community, are both important factors in closing the gap in protocol between European nations.

**Figure 1.12** Hands of foils holding tubes: the preparation of material for a scent-identification lineup in the Netherlands. (KLPD, 2002)

A scent-identification lineup can be used in a criminal investigation by the police or as evidence in a court trial. In the first case, the police are limited in their actions by human rights and by local law. In Western Europe, one may not violate the integrity of the human body, and police need to keep in mind that a person does not have to cooperate with the scent-identification lineup process if it will lead to his or her conviction. Collecting blood for an investigation, for example, would not be condoned in Western European countries. However, suspects usually do have to cooperate to provide hand odor. This is regulated by law, and in the Netherlands it is called a "measure in the interest of the investigation" and regarded as being similar to taking a picture or collecting a fingerprint.

In terms of scent-identification lineup results used as evidence in court trials, each country has its own particular set of laws and regulations. In countries that have jury-based courts, there are usually strict limits about what can be presented as evidence and what cannot. The Frye standard is often applied. According to this test, which determines the admissibility of scientific evidence presented in court, the following questions need to be answered: Is the method verifiable? Has it been tested, peer reviewed, and published? Does it have a known error rate? Is it standardized? Is it generally accepted?

Although Frye's points have not been cleared up completely for such generally accepted evidence as fingerprints and ballistics, new types of evidence are often scrutinized along these lines. Taslitz wrote a long essay on this topic reviewing the status of scent lineups and called their results an "unscientific myth."[14] In a book on the use of scientific evidence in judicial proceedings, the Polish scientist Wójcikiewicz also reviewed the status of scent identifications according to the Frye standard. He does not think all of Frye's points have been met for scent lineups, but he notes that the method tends to be favorably perceived.[15] However, if the situation in Europe continues in the direction it has taken now, and more scientists get involved in research and improvements, it will not be very long before scent-identification lineups meet all the criteria required for the Frye standard to be met, and the method can be presented as evidence in all countries that have adopted Frye as the standard.

## International Standards

Countries with a long tradition of the scent-identification lineup generally began by using it as a police investigation tool, using a single dog for quick results that could be discussed with the suspect. This conversation would often lead to a confession, which could then be presented in court. Gradually the method became more accepted and more frequently mentioned as the motivation for verdicts. Such is the case in the Netherlands, where research eventually led to significant improvements in official methods and protocols.

**Figure 1.13** Dutch standard: case with material for a scent-identification lineup. (KLPD, 2002)

Specially trained dogs investigate human scent-identification lineups as a part of police investigations, primarily to establish whether or not an individual has been at the scene of a crime. However, there is no international protocol on how these dogs are trained. In a step toward greater acceptance of scent identification performed by dogs, in 2016, French researchers published their analysis of data about dogs' performance in scent-identification tasks, provided since 2003 by the Division of the Technical and Scientific Police in Écully, France.[16]

To collect body scent (BS) for lineups, researchers asked individuals to hold two cotton squares for 10 minutes, and then place the squares in a sterile glass jar. When collecting trace scent (TS), researchers placed up to five cotton squares in direct contact with objects or clothes, then wrapped them together in aluminum foil for at least one hour. All cotton squares were then placed in one jar.

The researchers' results show that, at the end of an approximately two-year training program, the dogs were able to recognize the smell of an individual (matching BS to BS, and TS to TS) in 80 to 90 percent of cases and never mistake one smell for that of another person. However, the sensitivity scores obtained when the dogs were set to match BS to TS, and TS to BS, ranged from 71 to 74 percent. The fact that the dogs' ability to perform human-odor lineups was significantly greater when the type of odor (for example, that of a human hand) in the sample and in the lineup were the same (and stored in the same type of jar) clearly suggests that comparison between two odor samples of the same kind is much easier for dogs than comparison between two odor samples of different kinds.

This topic, however, needs to be investigated further. The researchers conducting this study collected all their scent samples on the same day. It would be interesting, and informative, to ask the dogs to match materials collected on different days, so "old" to "fresh," or vice versa, as is done in Dutch scent-discrimination lineups.[17]

There are some problematic aspects to the researchers' study, especially as it relates to the protocol used for the tests. The handler, of course, should not know which jar in the lineup holds the matching scent and must therefore stand with his or her back to the proceedings so as not to influence the dog's investigation of the scents. Dogs can, you see, learn to interpret the smallest body movements as cues. (This learning of unintentional human cues is called the Clever Hans Effect, which you can read about it in the next chapter of this book.) The dog can pick up on cues from other humans in the room, too. So, the helper who has put the odors in the different jars and knows which jar is correct should not stand in the same room and watch the dog's work, either. Still, this helper must be the one to signal whether or not the dog has found the match. In the Dutch protocol, the helper who creates the lineup does so in a different room, and he or she also observes the lineup investigation from a different room, watching through a window and indicating incorrect or correct matches by flashing a red or green light.

Furthermore, in this study, it is unclear how the helper creates the lineup—all we know is that he or she put the odors "at random" in jars. Does the helper follow a certain protocol, or is there a risk that the "correct" scent might be found too often in the same place in the lineup? Does the helper first bring in the foil scents, and then the target scent—the dog will pick up on such a pattern. Finally, the French study does not seem to include testing the dogs to find out if they have a preference for the target scent, which is a key part of the Dutch scent-identification protocol.

We agree with the researchers when they say, "Despite the great ability shown by dogs in lineup tasks, the method has not gained widespread recognition in the worldwide forensic community, and human scent-identification results remain a controversial form of legal evidence. One reason for reluctance to use this method seems to be a lack of international standards for the way in which dogs are trained, certified and used."

To encourage adoption of an international standard, we strongly advise all handlers and police teams to use the considered and scientifically tested Dutch protocol for human scent-identification lineups, which takes into consideration all of the questions posed above.

# 2

# The Dutch Training Method for Scent Identification

The training method outlined in this chapter is the way dogs in the Canine Unit of the Netherlands National Police Force are trained to perform scent-identification lineups. Dogs at the Dutch Canine Unit are generally trained according to the so-called tube-retrieving method. This means human scents are collected on stainless steel tubes, and these tubes are clamped onto a platform. The tube that the dog indicates is released if it is a correct indication; an incorrect indication is never rewarded with a release of the tube.

## Scent-Identification Equipment and Room

Human odors are collected on square stainless steel tubes. The tubes are four inches (10 cm) long and almost one inch (2 cm) square. After use, the tubes are placed in a holder and washed in a dishwasher using ordinary detergent at the highest temperature 203ºF (95ºC). After that, they are boiled in clean water for another hour. They are allowed to dry and then put into glass jars with twist-off tops. The tubes are scented by asking a person to open the jar, take the tubes out, and hold them in their hands. After about one minute, the person is asked to return the tubes to the glass jar and close the lid. The jar is labeled and the tubes are ready for use.

The platforms used in the Netherlands are made of wood and coated with material that prevents the dog from slipping. Each platform is about one yard (1 m) wide and six yards (5.5 m) long. Seven stainless steel plates are lined up down the middle of the platform, with 20 inches (50 cm) in between each one. The plates can be removed for thorough cleaning, which is done in a dishwasher. Each plate is six by 14 inches (15 by 35 cm) and has a construction built on them to hold the tubes.

In Figure 2.2, the plate is shown in light gray; the fixed parts are black. The tube is placed on the fixed structures. The tubes are taken from the glass jar using clean tongs and put on the plate with these same tongs. A switch fixes the tube into place. After the dog has responded to a matching tube, it can be released with the same switch. The probe moves to the right, releasing the tube, which can then be picked up by the dog. The mechanism that moves the probes is located underneath the platform and connected to a switchbox near the handler. Each location is numbered, as are the switches, so each plate can be operated independently. Each time the platforms are used, the plates are sprayed with clean water and wiped clean.

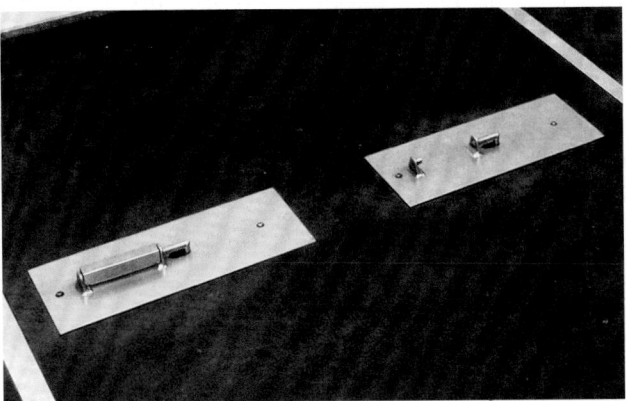

**Figure 2.1** Tube clamping device on the scent identification platform.

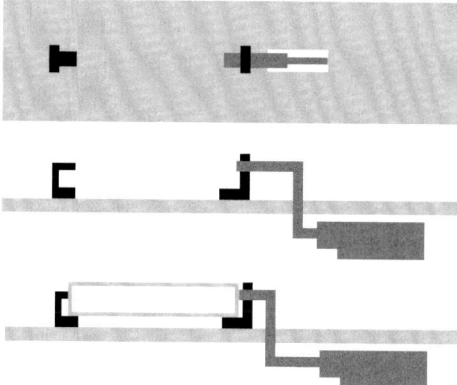

**Figure 2.2** The tube clamping device. From top to bottom: view from the top of the platform; section view from the side in released state without tube; section view from the side with tube clamped in place.

Two platforms are located in a room approximately three yards (3 m) from each other. Each platform has its own switchbox to operate the probes that fix the tubes. The room is regularly cleaned with ordinary detergents and then aired. The wooden platforms themselves are also cleaned regularly.

One wall in the room has a one-way mirror that allows observation from outside. Besides the platforms and the switch boxes, the room has a whiteboard to register the location of the odors on the platform, a table or shelf to hold the glass jars with the tubes, and a red/green signaling system connected to the observation room. This is used when the handler works blind and does not know the position of the matching tube. The person in the observation room uses the light to signal whether the dog's choice is correct or not.

## Training in Six Phases

Training consists of six phases based on the composition of odors in the lineup and the matches the dog has to make (Figure 2.3).

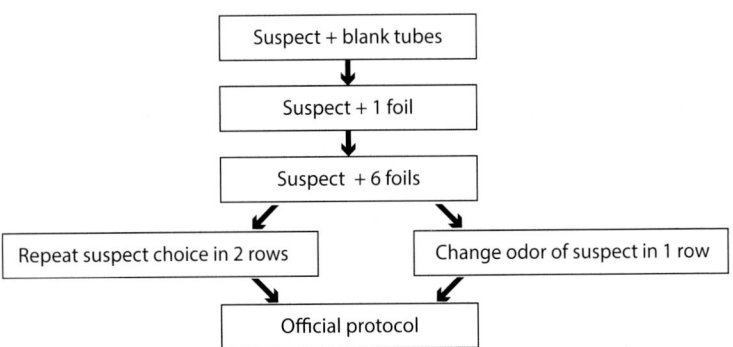

**Figure 2.3** The six phases of scent-identification lineup training.

In the first three phases, the composition of the row is made progressively more complex: from a single scented tube in the midst of unscented tubes in phase 1 to seven different, equally scented tubes in phase 3. In the last three phases, the matches the dog has to make are trained up to the level of the official scent-identification lineup procedure in the Netherlands, in which a first match has to be repeated in a second row of tubes (the control test), and then a second match with a new odor has to be made within the same lineup procedure (the scent lineup).

### BUILDING UP COMPLEXITY

The building up of the odors in the row from unscented tubes to seven different odors is done as follows. In phase 1, the odor of the suspect is presented in the midst of unscented tubes. In phase 2, the odor of the suspect is presented in the midst of tubes that have been scented by one other person. In phase 3, the odor of the suspect is presented amidst tubes scented by different people.

Up to this stage, usually the matches have been made on a single platform with a single line of tubes. Besides increasing the number of scents in the row, the articles the dog is presented as sample, or smeller, are varied in the course of these phases. The final result of phase 3 must be that the dog reliably makes a match based on a reasonable variety of well (hand-) scented articles in a row of tubes that have been prepared in a similar way at the same time.

Training the dog further for the official protocol begins in phase 4. Two rows are now used, and the choice the dog makes in row 1 is repeated in row 2. In phase 5, the odor the dog has to search for is changed in a single row: first one person is the suspect, then a second person. Phases 4 and 5 can be trained at the same time, alternating each one.

In phase 6, the official protocol is trained: first selecting the odor of one control suspect in two rows, then selecting the odor of a second suspect in both rows.

### GENERAL GUIDELINES

The different phases are described in more detail below with a goal and timeframe for each one. The training plan is based on approximately three sessions a day, five days a week. After the goal and timeframe, the general training method is described along with tips to solve specific training problems that can occur during this phase in the training.

The phases as described below should be seen as general guidelines for the training. In reality, phases will not be as clearly separated, and it is even advisable to go back a phase regularly. A general rule is that before a new phase is introduced, let the dog make a choice at a familiar level first. For example, before starting phase 3 training, let the dog do one or two searches at phase 2. Only when the dog no longer makes mistakes at phase 2 should you start a training session at a higher level.

### PHASE 1: THE DOG LEARNS TO SEARCH FOR A SCENTED TUBE AMIDST UNSCENTED ONES

**Goal:** The dog takes scent from a scented object or tube (hereafter called the smeller). The row consists of seven tubes, one of which has been scented by the same person that scented the smeller. The dog searches in the row for the scented tube and ignores the

**Figure 2.4** Phase 1 training: a scented tube is hidden behind one of the large unscented objects in the row on the platform.

unscented ones. He persists in his choice. This has to be performed correctly at least five times.

**Timeframe:** Maximum of two weeks.

**Method:** Before each choice, the dog is given the smeller to smell. Subsequent sessions:

1. In view of the dog, a tube is hidden in a row of seven heavy objects. By hiding the tube, you stimulate the dog to use his nose. After a period of time, the tube is hidden while the dog cannot see it, or the dog is misled by pretending to hide the tube in another place in the row. At first the tubes are "warm" and put into the row by the person who scented the tubes; later on they are "cold" (up to two days old).

2. Unscented tubes are added to the row of heavy objects. It is best to do this after the dog has already made a choice as described in the previous exercise, since the dog then already knows which odor he is after. The unscented tubes should be fixed so the dog cannot retrieve an incorrect tube. After

some time, the scented tube should also be fixed to teach the dog to persist in his choice.

3. Now the objects are removed from the row. All tubes are fixed. The dog must walk along the row of tubes and make a choice. Praise the dog for a correct choice, or physically reward him with vigorous petting before the tube clamp is opened and he is rewarded. The dog must make his choice independently. At first, praise the dog immediately so he knows he's made a correct choice. Slowly create a time interval between the first response of the dog and the first reaction of the handler. This is necessary for future blind work where there will be an interval between when the dog makes his choice and when he receives his reward. The dog must learn from the start that he must persist in his choice.

## PHASE 2: THE DOG LEARNS TO SEARCH FOR THE SUSPECT'S TUBE AMIDST TUBES SCENTED BY ONE OTHER PERSON

**Goal:** The dog takes scent from the smeller. The row consists of seven tubes scented in a similar manner and at the same time: one tube has been scented by the same person who has scented the smeller. The other six tubes are scented by one other person. The dog searches for the tube with the matching odor of the smeller. He persists in his choice. This must be conducted correctly at least five consecutive times.

**Timeframe:** Maximum of two weeks.

**Method:** There are two main training methods for this phase:

1. Method using "older foils": the tubes of the foil are much older (this means they have been scented several months/weeks/days earlier) than those of the suspect. An intermediate phase can consist of first letting the dog make a choice in a row of one suspect tube and blank tubes and repeating this choice in a row where the blank tubes have been replaced by tubes scented one month earlier, for example. Gradually the age of the foil's tubes can be decreased until they are scented at the same time as the suspect's tubes.

2. Method using "weaker foils": the tubes of the foils are scented for a much shorter time than the tubes of the suspect. An intermediate phase can consist of first letting the dog make a choice in a row of one suspect tube and blank tubes and repeating this choice in a row where the blank tubes have been replaced by tubes scented briefly, for a couple of seconds, for example. Gradually the duration of scenting the foil's tubes can be increased until they are scented equally as long as the suspect's tubes.

A disadvantage of both methods is that the dog may learn to look for the "odd tube" in the row: the freshest odor, or the strongest, or the odor of which there is only one in the row, and so on. It is necessary to pass through these phases quickly to prevent the dog from fixing on this strategy. Otherwise, the dog's fixation will be a nuisance later in the training, when he must be taught not to follow it.

### PHASE 3: THE DOG LEARNS TO SEARCH FOR THE ODOR OF THE SUSPECT IN A COMPLETE ROW

**Goal:** The dog takes scent from the smeller. The row consists of seven tubes that have been scented in a similar manner and at the same time: one tube has been scented by the same person that scented the smeller; the other six tubes have been scented by six different people. The dog persists in his choice. The dog must stabilize at this level and for two weeks attain an average of 80 percent correct in his first choice.

**Timeframe:** Approximately three months.

**Method:** Both methods described in phase 2 can be extended:

1. Method using "older foils": once the dog can make a correct choice amidst tubes scented by a single foil, the odor of a second foil can be introduced in the row. If this creates a problem, an intermediate phase is to let the tubes of the foils be a little older than those of the suspect. It is not necessary to revert to much older tubes; usually a day or two difference

is sufficient to solve this problem. If the dog makes correct choices when a single tube of a second foil is included in the row, more tubes of this second foil can be introduced.

2. Method using "weaker foils": once the dog can make a correct choice amidst tubes scented by a single foil, the odor of a second foil can be introduced in the row. If this creates a problem, an intermediate phase is to let the tubes of the foils be a little weaker than the tubes of the suspect.

The step from smelling one to six different foils is relatively simple for the dog, and the use of repetition makes the introduction of new scents easy for the dog to adjust. The tube of the suspect can first be placed in position 2 or 3, allowing the dog to come across only one or two other odors before reaching the correct tube. When repeating the choice, the suspect's tube can be placed somewhere farther along, leading the dog to smell many different odors before reaching the correct tube. After the dog has performed this successfully several times, the position of the choices *must* be random (throw a die to choose them) to prevent the dog from building up expectations.

It is fully possible that the odor of a particular person is difficult for a dog, or that the odor of one of the foils is particularly attractive for a dog, or that the tubes have not been scented well, or that the dog's nose is not working optimally on a particular day. Stability means 80 percent correct, counting only first choices.

The dog must learn to handle mistakes: not to panic, but to continue searching when she is given a verbal reprimand. Accept non-recognitions from your dog. Also accept mistakes and try to analyze where they come from. If the dog reacts strongly to one of the foils, remove this foil from the row. The downside to using force to reprimand is that the dog will start paying attention to the handler, looking for cues to prevent the handler from punishing her. She will stop using her nose when this happens.

## PHASE 4: THE DOG LEARNS TO MAKE REPETITIONS IN TWO ROWS

**Goal:** The dog takes scent from a smeller. Now there are two rows of seven odors each: one of the suspect and six of different foils. The dog is given scent from the smeller in front of each row and must respond to the odor of the suspect in both rows. The dog must learn to work correctly in both rows and persist in her choice.

**Timeframe:** Alternating with phase 5, approximately four months.

**Method:** Logical continuation of phase 3. The dog must learn to go from one row to the other. She has to learn to take scent from a smeller in front of each row.

## PHASE 5: THE DOG LEARNS TO CHANGE SUSPECTS WITHIN A ROW

**Goal:** The dog takes scent from a smeller and matches it to the correct tube in a row consisting of seven different odors. After this he is given scent from a second smeller scented by a different person. A matching tube is already present in the row, and the dog learns to make this second match.

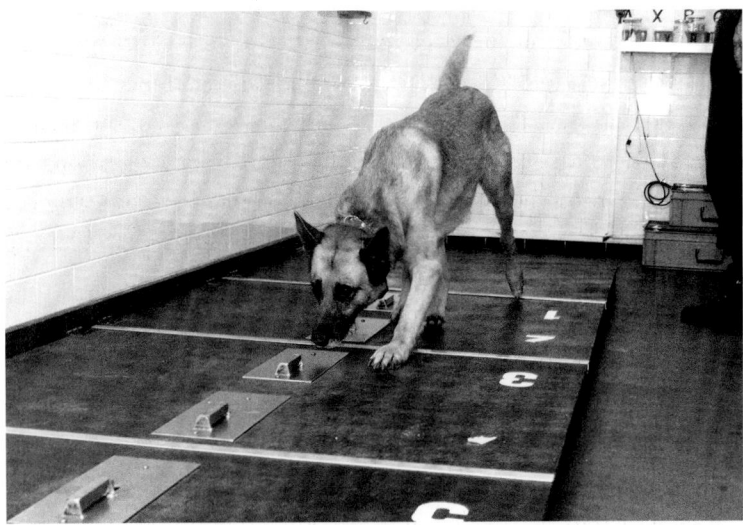

**Figure 2.5** The dog searches the row of tubes.

**Timeframe:** Alternating with phase 4, approximately four months.
**Method:** After a correct first choice, the dog is given a second smeller. In the beginning, this is a scented tube or another object the dog has no difficulty with. Later, both choices are based on different kinds of objects. This exercise can easily be expanded to three or four different objects (scented by different people), thus "emptying the platform" as the dog progressively matches a smeller with each scent in the row.

If a dog cannot make a choice, switch to another odor using an easier object or adding a scented tube to the object. Always ensure you have enough material when starting a run; plan ahead in case an exercise doesn't work out.

If the first choice is difficult for the dog, fall back to phase 3 and repeat the choice a number of times instead of switching odors. In the beginning, a dog will experience more difficulty changing odors after a number of repetitions. Switch to another odor only if the first choice was nicely performed.

If changing odors continues to be difficult for the dog, try letting the second choice be made in a second, very short row consisting of only three or four tubes. In this way the choice is limited and hopefully easier for the dog. If this goes well, then the second choice can be repeated in the first long row. Other suggestions are to leave the room between choices one and two to let the dog get a "fresh nose" or hiding the second object somewhere and letting the dog use his nose to find it.

### PHASE 6: THE DOG LEARNS TO WORK FOLLOWING THE OFFICIAL PROTOCOL
**Goal:** The dog takes scent from the first smeller and searches for the matching odor in two different rows. After this he takes scent from the second smeller, and searches for the matching odor in the same two rows. The dog must become experienced in different types of smellers, duration and time of scenting of the objects, aged

objects, and additional smells of an object. His performance must stabilize: choices of "fresh" objects must be 80 percent correct during a month. Then one can apply for certification.

**Timeframe:** The remainder of his working life.

**Method:** The dog is given the second smeller only if the first odor was chosen quickly and correctly. In the beginning, these second smellers must be easy objects for the dog, later more difficult ones can be given. When certain objects, particular additional smells, or older scents create a problem for the dog, an intermediate phase is to let these be scented by someone familiar and friendly to the dog. A second intermediate phase is to let such an object be scented by a person unknown to the dog, but from whom it is certain that the dog is able to correctly identify based on "normal" objects.

## Certification

In the Netherlands, dogs and handlers taking part in a scent-identification task must be certified by the Dutch Minister of Justice and Minister of the Interior. Certifications last for two years and ensure that dogs and handlers, as a team, are up to the tasks required of them. Certifications ensure that the risk of mistakes is kept to a minimum. Each dog's certificate records the kind of scent-carriers the dog works with, the presentation method of these scent-carriers (typically a stainless steel tube), the response of the dog to a match, and his reward. The dog's performance at each lineup is also recorded.

## The Dutch Protocol for Scent-Identification Lineups

In this protocol, the odor of the suspect (called "odor X") is one of seven different odors. Each of these seven odors is present in two rows, but in a different sequence. Five of the odors in both rows are from foils. The seventh odor belongs to a control person (called "odor A"). The position of the odors is random. The handler does not know which odors belong to the suspect or the control person.

## SEQUENCE SCHEMES FOR SCENT LINEUPS

The 1997 Dutch protocol for scent-identification lineups ensures objectivity in the sequence the odors of the suspect and the foils are presented to the dog. To select the order, the helper throws a die twice, creating a two-figure number. This number is found in the scheme below, and the odors (coded as X for the suspect, A for the control odor, and B to F for the foils) then are placed on the platform according to the matching scheme.

| | | |
|---|---|---|
| 11 A X B E C F D<br>C D X F A B E | 21 E D B X C A F<br>D C A F B E X | 31 B A D X C F E<br>D E B F C X A |
| 12 D E X A B F C<br>B A F D C E X | 22 B C X D A F E<br>E B C D F A X | 32 C E B X A F D<br>C A B E X D F |
| 13 E B X C F A D<br>C E B A F D X | 23 E B C F X A D<br>A B F C X D E | 33 E D C F X A B<br>F B A X E D C |
| 14 E X A B F C D<br>B E A F X C D | 24 B C X A F E D<br>A E B C X F D | 34 X A B F C D E<br>F C D E A X B |
| 15 F E D B C X A<br>B C A E X F D | 25 D F A B E X C<br>X D F C E B A | 35 B X A D C E F<br>A X F E D C B |
| 16 X C B A F D E<br>A D X F C E B | 26 F B C X E A D<br>B F E D C X A | 36 D C F B E X A<br>A D F X B C E |
| 41 C F X E B A D<br>A X B C F E D | 51 X F D C B E A<br>C A X F D B E | 61 F A C X B D E<br>X A B F D E C |
| 42 D E B F A C X<br>X A B C F D E | 52 X A B C E F D<br>F E A X B D C | 62 B X F C E D A<br>E F B A C D X |
| 43 F E D A B C X<br>B E X D C A F | 53 C B A D X F E<br>X F E C A D B | 63 A C B F X D E<br>D X E B C F A |
| 44 D X B F A C E<br>B C D A E X F | 54 A B C D E F X<br>D C X B A F E | 64 A D F E B X C<br>X B C A E F D |
| 45 X E F B A C D<br>B A D X F E C | 55 E A C B D F X<br>D E F X B A C | 65 C E A D X B F<br>E X B C D A F |
| 46 F E X A B C D<br>C D E F A B X | 56 C D E X F B A<br>E C F A D X B | 66 A C E B D X F<br>D X B F E C A |

Before the dog is allowed to compare the odor of the *corpus delicti* with the odors in the rows, the ability of the dog to perform scent-identification lineups is tested by searching for the scent of the control person in both rows. By doing this, the dog also shows that he has no preference for or special interest in the odor of the suspect. If the dog responds to another odor than that of the control person and thus makes an incorrect choice, the dog is disqualified. If the dog does not respond to any odor and has smelled all the carriers, the handler recalls his dog. This also leads to a disqualification, which means the procedure is stopped.

If his dog positively identifies the control person in both rows (steps 1 and 2), the handler must evaluate the behavior of the dog in both rows (step 3). If the handler concludes that his dog has shown special interest in one of the odors in a row, he must let the helper know. If this odor belongs to the suspect, the dog is disqualified for the remainder of the lineup. If the odor did not belong to the suspect, the lineup may continue.

In steps 4 and 5, the dog may compare the odor of the *corpus delicti* with the remaining six odors in each row. If the dog responds only to the odor of the suspect and ignores all the other odors, this is a *positive identification*. If the dog responds to the odor of one of the foils, the helper lets the handler know this is wrong, and the lineup is terminated. The conclusion of this lineup is reported as *incorrect procedure*. If the dog does not respond to any of the odors but has smelled all of them, the conclusion that will be reported is *no odor similarity*.

## Scent Lineup Training Tips

Scent-identification lineup work requires a dog to search for a matching odor independently and full of concentration. Performing this work has to be a fun activity for the dog with his handler. A lack of motivation can be influenced by the relationship between dog and handler, and also by physical influences (back pain, sore foot, ear infection, in heat, or a bitch in heat in the neighborhood). Establish the cause of a lack of motivation, have patience, and adjust your training.

## OVERVIEW OF THE DUTCH SCENT-IDENTIFICATION LINEUP PROCEDURE

| Step | Row | Starter Object | Choice by Dog | Result |
|------|-----|----------------|---------------|--------|
| 1 | 1 | control object (odor A) | A (control person) | continue with 2 |
|   |   |   | B, C, D, E, F or X (suspect) | disqualified |
|   |   |   | no response | disqualified |
| 2 | 2 | control object (odor A) | A (control person) | continue with 3 |
|   |   |   | B, C, D, E, F or X (suspect) | disqualified |
|   |   |   | no response | disqualified |
| 3 | 1 & 2 |   | no interest for odor of X (suspect) | continue with 4 |
|   |   |   | interest for odor of X (suspect) | disqualified |
| 4 | 1 | *corpus delicti* | X (suspect) | continue with 5 |
|   |   |   | B, C, D, E or F | incorrect procedure |
|   |   |   | no response | no odor similarity |
| 5 | 2 | *corpus delicti* | X (suspect) | odor similarity |
|   |   |   | B, C, D, E or F | incorrect procedure |
|   |   |   | no response | no odor similarity |

One cannot force a dog to do scent-identification lineups: coercion only leads to a dog paying attention to the handler instead of to the scent involved. The dog has to enjoy the game, otherwise it is better to stop. Some dogs prefer other activities, such as tracking or detection work. If that's the case, there is no point in forcing the work.

## Systematic Issues in Training

In training, a dog can learn to react to many types of systematic oddities, as when the matching odor in the lineup is always collected last, or when this person is asked to give odor for a longer period of time. This leads to the scent picture of the matching odor being fresher, or stronger, than the other odors in the lineup. If this is done consistently, the dog can learn to react to this difference, since following this "fresh, strong odor" strategy leads to a reward. Dutch police dog handlers are aware of this danger and take sufficient precautions, which are also part of the official regulations.

Another systematic mistake that a dog can pick up is if the odors of the foils are always laid out first, with the matching odor added last. Dogs are sensitive to time and concentration differences; it appears they find the direction in a track by noticing differences in concentration between one footstep and another. If the matching odor is systematically added to the lineup last, a dog will learn to respond to this cue without you even realizing it.

In training, avoid these kinds of consistent differences in treatment between the matching odor and the foil odors. If you don't, we may think the dog is working well, but he may in fact be using quite different cues than the "matching odor" cue we want him to use. A slightly different procedure may bring this problem to light, and once we discover the dogs have learned to use an unintended cue, we are thrown way back in training. The only cue the dog should be able to use is the "matching odor" cue. Design your training to ensure you are not unintentionally cuing the dog improperly.

Another problem in training: if the odor of one of the kennel staff is present in the lineup, dogs may respond strongly to this person's odor, particularly if the person is well liked by the dog for providing food, walks, and attention. Some dogs will keep returning to this person's scent. Trying to get the dog to ignore the scent in the same lineup will only lead to the dog paying attention to the handler. We always advise avoiding the inclusion of the odor of such a person in a lineup. If it is unclear why the dog is reacting to a specific odor, then it is better to remove this scent from the lineup before continuing.

We saw training in which a number of dogs showed a strong preference for position 5. It became clear that this position preference was a result of improper training. The handlers of these dogs did not place the position of the matching tube randomly, but instead chose it themselves. The logic they used was that later positions in the row required the dog to ignore a number of odors, demonstrating that he was working well and not responding to the first odor he came across, before reaching the matching tube. Their result was teaching the dogs that they'd often choose correctly at tube 5. It is far better to choose the tube position randomly, as per our recommended method using a die.

### PROBLEMS TAKING THE SCENT

In order to be able to associate the odor on the smeller to the odor in the row, the dog must pick up scent from the smeller very well. However, smelling the object cannot be forced, so you must be able to stimulate the dog's attention for the object. In order to do that, you can start outdoors in coupling the smelling of an article in a searching game. For example, after the dog has smelled at an object, throw it so the dog can retrieve it. Later on the object can be hidden, and the dog may locate it by smell and retrieve it.

In another method, you can hide the smeller object before the lineup in one of three jars. Let the dog first locate the object there, and reward him for finding it, perhaps by letting an unscented tube "magically" appear out of this jar that he can then retrieve. By immediately letting this exercise be followed by a scent-identification lineup using this same object as the smeller, the coupling of the odor on the object and the odor on the tube becomes clear.

For dogs that don't like to take scent from the smeller, you can place the smeller object on the ground in front of the platform and let the dog lie down near it. Ignore the dog; he will eventually smell at the object by himself. This may take time; have patience.

### PROBLEMS WORKING ON THE PLATFORM

Finding the matching tube is easier for the dog if he walks down the line of tubes at a reasonable pace and takes his time to smell each tube. Some dogs do this by nature, but most don't. "Fast" dogs need to be slowed down from the beginning, when the choices they have to make are still fairly simple. Begin by letting the dog lie down in front of the row after giving him the scent. Stroke the dog until he is relaxed. Very calmly, let him go. It is best to have the dog lying immediately in front of the platform: if he is lying at a distance, he can build up speed while approaching the platform.

In another method, you can slow down the dog using a leash. The dog must be used to working on leash before you can do this because he must not experience the leash as a punishment. By letting the leash slip gently, you can regulate the speed of the dog. The downside to this method is that by "braking" the dog continuously, the dog may react by pulling, which only increases his speed.

You can also try this method: instead of starting the dog at the head of the platform near tube 1, start the dog at the side of the platform. This means the dog has to turn at the first tube he encounters, which slows him down.

Both a steady pace on the platform and working systematically from position 1 to 7 facilitate the dog's ability to choose. In order to reach this steady pace, you can guide the dog by hand to the first position on the platform and after that calmly to the next tubes. Another possibility is letting someone else tap the platform near position 1 to focus the attention of the dog towards the first position and after that slowly to the next positions.

Some dogs have a tendency to turn before they reach the end of the lineup, often on position 6. This can be the result of prior conditioning, of a rhythm developed earlier, or a training system in which too many matching tubes were placed at the beginning of the lineup, which resulted in the dog's expectation that the matching tube is somewhere in the beginning of the row. In order to avoid this problem, place the matching tube at the back of the lineup a number of times in an easy choice, such as one scented tube amidst blank, unscented tubes, so that the dog can do her own searching without you having to "help" her. Let the dog figure it out by herself, but do not put the matching tube at the end of the row too often, since this will only shift the problem. You can also put the matching tube down randomly, but have someone pretend to place it at the end of the lineup while the dog is watching.

It can also be helpful to walk down the lineup with the dog, but do this in all situations, even when the matching tube is in the beginning of the lineup. Gradually increase the distance between you and the dog so that the possible pressure on the dog because of your presence is less.

### NEGATIVE EXPERIENCES

A dog must continue to search in spite of a soft verbal correction. If a dog becomes nervous, he is not searching well anymore but instead paying attention to its handler. The basic trust between dog and handler must be built up outside scent-identification training. A mistake on the scent-identification platform is not self-rewarding since the dog is not rewarded with a tube. This makes it possible to correct the dog verbally.

When a dog has had a number of negative experiences on the platform, he may show several kinds of behavior: pacing nervously up and down, avoiding the lineup, or moving in such a way that he can keep an eye on the handler.

It is important to first establish the cause of this behavior. Have mistakes been made during the preparation of the lineup, such as the suspect's odor being placed incorrectly, or using poorly scented tubes? Has the handler had an off day and reacted too sharply? Does the dog have a sensitive nature? The solution can only be found if the cause of the problem is determined.

The usual solution is to make the lineup easier by using the odor of a familiar person or using an easy article as a smeller, but beware of the danger of always reverting to a scented tube or by preparing a "short" row with only a few odors or a row with only one scented tube.

## PROBLEMS WITH ODOR RECOGNITION

A dog may suddenly have problems making recognitions for many reasons, such as when the training has always followed a standard form and suddenly "new" things are introduced, such as completely different articles or articles that have been scented earlier. Several suggestions to solve odor recognition problems follow.

- First, use the odors of people the dog is familiar with.
- If an object went particularly well, and you see the person who scented it on a regular basis, keep the article well packed and collect fresh tubes from this person regularly.

In general, matching identical objects such as tube as smeller to tubes in lineup, or cloth as smeller and cloths in lineup is easy for dogs. The transition to matching different kinds of objects can be a problem. This transition can be stimulated in different ways:

- Combine the scent of an article with the scent on a tube as a smeller for the first match.
- First give the dog scent from a tube, then from an object so the dog is given the opportunity to "recognize" the scent from the tube on the object.
- Select articles that contain metal parts when matches are made with scents on tubes.
- If a dog has not made a match (but also no mistake), give the dog a tube containing the scent he should be looking for. Then again give scent from the article and let him make the match in the lineup.
- If a dog has made a match using one of the above tips, keep the article and tubes of this person and use them again after a short while for a new match. This time, only present the article as smeller.

- If a dog has problems with recognitions but does make a correct choice, it is very important to teach the dog to persist in his choice with strong verbal encouragement.

## NON-RECOGNITIONS

Not making a match can be the result of accepting and rewarding a "non-recognition" too often or too elaborately. For example, the dog walks up and down the row, going through the motions, and cheerfully returns to the handler for his reward. In this case, it can help to walk the line up and down with the dog. The dog will be paying attention to the handler in this case, so the choices need to be simple.

Sometimes it helps to simply take the dog away and put him in his kennel when he has not made a match: a "time out." This makes some dogs more eager to work and more willing to make a choice the next time.

## BUILDING UP THE TRAINING TIME INTERVAL

During training, the dog is usually rewarded quickly because a quick reward stimulates the learning process. However, when later on the handler works "blind," the time interval between the response of the dog and his reward becomes greater. After a dog has made a choice, the handler has to signal, is given a signal back, and only then can the reward be given. This causes a time interval.

A dog that expects a quick response can experience this time lapse as "incorrect" and so the dog may not persist in his choice. Therefore it is important to train the dog to persist in his choice early on in training. Deliberately increase the time between the response of the dog and the first verbal praise by the handler. Or when the dog has made her choice, reward her by petting her near the tube she has chosen, stimulating her to stay with her choice.

- If the dog reacts to the correct tube, but does not stay there, simply take the dog away and put her in her kennel without comment or reward. For some dogs this works well: it makes them more eager and this makes them persist in their choice the next time.

- Poor recognitions can also be the result of a physical problem. Even the beginning of an infection such as kennel cough can lead to a diminished sense of smell. Scale on teeth or poor breath can also lead to problems. Oncoming heat, or being in heat, can affect both the sense of smell and concentration. A bitch in heat in the neighborhood or changes in the pack order can also affect dogs.

# 3

# Dogs' Responsiveness to Human Gestures

Everyone who has ever tried to teach a dog something knows that dogs respond very well to handler cues. Most people will also realize that dogs pick up cues that they were not specifically trained in. For example, if you put on your walking shoes, your dog will stick to you like glue because he expects to go for a walk. The question is how subtle the cues can be and whether dogs can pick up cues you yourself are completely unconscious of. The results of these unconscious kinds of cues are called the Clever Hans Effect, named after the apparent mathematic abilities of a horse called Hans.

## The Clever Hans Effect

Clever Hans was a stallion that lived at the turn of the 20th century in Germany. His behavior racked the brains of the animal psychologists of his time, made a name for a pattern, and still is of importance in training dogs. The owner of this horse, Wilhelm von Osten, was an eccentric man with a peculiar idea. He believed that a horse is at least as intelligent as a human. He was absolutely convinced that horses could count, read, and think. To prove it, he set to work.

The first thing he did was to give his horse Hans a certain "language." After careful consideration, he chose the tapping of the horse's front hoof as the mechanism for communication. All letters in the alphabet and every number were each represented by a specific number of hoof tappings. As he began training Hans in this language, Von Osten took Hans's leg in his hands and tapped it for him. The horse eventually learned to move his leg without help, and after some time the animal seemed to understand this language.

On June 28, 1902, in a paper called *Militärwochenblatt,* an advertisement appeared with the following text:

> I want to sell my seven-year-old, fine, docile stallion with which I do tests in order to determine the intellectual powers of a horse. The horse distinguishes ten colors, reads, knows the four main processes of calculation, and a lot more. Von Osten, Griebenowstrasse 10, Berlin.

"A lot more" included spelling, as well as knowledge of musical notes, coins, cards, and how to tell the time. But Von Osten did not really want to sell Hans. His advertisement was meant to garner interest in his horse and gain popularity for his opinion that animals are creatures with keen minds. To the annoyance of Wilhelm von Osten, nobody responded to his advertisement as it was believed to be a late April Fool's joke.

### A MIRACULOUS HORSE

Only after a second advertisement did Von Osten receive a response. Now it was time to show off Hans's capabilities to a select group of invited guests, who were allowed to interrogate Hans. The horse proved to know a lot. Hans could name the date, tell what time it was, convert fractions into decimal numbers, add up, subtract, multiply, and divide in answer to guests' questions. The people present were amazed at the horse's abilities.

News of the Kluger Hans (Clever Hans) event went around the country, and even the world press wrote about it. A lot of people thought Hans's performance was somehow fraudulent, but reports of the event were so impressive that animal psychologists became

**Figure 3.1** The stallion Clever Hans and his owner and trainer Mr. Wilhelm von Osten.

**Figure 3.2** Clever Hans during one of his performances.

enthusiastic and wanted to examine Hans. All were astonished because Wilhelm von Osten did not wish to capitalize on his miraculous horse.

A committee of leading scientists tested the horse, after which they did not take a specific position. They admitted they did not detect the kinds of tricks usually used in circuses with performing animals. The hesitation of the scientists shows how deceptively real Hans's skills were. On August 11, 1904, in the *Lokal-Anzeiger*, a Berlin newspaper, C.G. Schillings wrote in no uncertain terms: "I want to state that the stallion understands the German language, figures [does math] as about a 13-year-old child can, distinguishes a lot of different colors, correctly names geometric figures, correctly indicates musical notes, knows melodies and their names, and reacts unlimitedly to questions just like a human...."

## MINOR MOVEMENTS
However, then animal psychologist Oskar Pfungst discovered the truth about Clever Hans. Pfungst precisely observed the way the horse worked and also carefully watched Von Osten. It was clear to him that there was no swindle—after all, Pfungst, all alone with the horse, questioned the stallion and the animal answered in the correct way with his tapping language. For a person without animal psychological training, there would be no doubt that the horse could indeed think and do math. A day after questioning Hans, Pfungst performed another experiment. He asked Hans questions that nobody present in the room knew the answer. The stallion started tapping his hoof and did not stop. As Pfungst wrote, "The animal seemed to be absentminded." It was clear that the stallion was waiting for a cue to stop tapping. But this sign couldn't be given because nobody present knew the answer to the question. Pfungst wrote:

> So far as I can see, the following explanation is the only one that will comport with these facts: The horse must have

**Figure 3.3** In 1910, the German animal psychologist Karl Krall teaches the horse Zarif to spell.

learned, in the course of the long period of problem-solving, to attend ever more closely, while tapping, to the slight changes in bodily posture with which the master unconsciously accompanied the steps in his own thought-processes, and to use these as closing signals. The motive for this direction and straining of attention was the regular reward, in the form of carrots and bread, which attended it. This unexpected kind of independent activity and the certainty and precision of the perception of minimal movements thus attained are astounding in the highest degree.

The movements that call forth the horse's reaction are so extremely slight in the case of Mr. Von Osten that it is easily comprehensible how it was possible that they should escape the notice even of practised observers.[1]

Pfungst stumbled across Hans's reaction to a small, unconscious movement with the head or the body of the questioner as soon as he reached the correct answer, and Hans used this as a cue to stop tapping.

## Clever Dog Nora

So, Wilhelm von Osten did not succeed in proving that the mental capacity of the horse is as good as that of the human. But his four years of laborious training produced evidence that an animal can take note of even slight human movements, gestures that people normally do not perceive.

Emilio Rendich, a painter, trained his dog Nora to respond in much the same way as Clever Hans. The dog would start responding, and when the correct figure was reached, Rendich would lean forward and Nora would stop. Unfortunately, Rendich's work is only described in a rather inaccessible and rare German book by K. Krall, published in 1912.[2] But Rendich showed that his dog, like Clever Hans, was capable of perceiving extremely subtle physical cues.

## Test with Signs

Dogs seem to be able to learn physical cues faster than Clever Hans did, as Hungarian Dr. Ádám Miklősi proved in his study of

**Figure 3.4** Excited by the reports about Clever Hans and Nora, people soon made attempts to teach other dogs new tricks. Paula Moeckel from the German city Mannheim was successful with her knock-speaking Airedale terrier Rolf, circa 1919.

this subject in 1998.[3] He explored whether or not dogs perceived and made use of the cues he displayed, such as pointing, bowing, nodding, head turning, and glancing. In his setup, the dog was positioned about 10 feet (3 m) in front of two pots, one of which contained food. The experimenter stood between the pots and gave the dog her cue, and then the dog could freely choose a bowl. Several of these sessions involved groups of dogs. Their performance in the first 15 trials was compared with that of the last 15 trials.

The first group of six dogs were 1.5 years old and in training to become disability assistant dogs. They all responded to the pointing cue without training. Most dogs in this group also responded to the bowing cue, and some learned to do so over the course of the experiment. Most dogs in the group also learned nodding quite easily. Head turning was more difficult for them; only three dogs managed to learn this. Finally, only one dog learned and responded to glancing.

The second group of dogs were older and had lived with families for a long time. These dogs had not received explicit training. During the experiment, they were trained to respond to the same gestures as the first group. All of these dogs responded to pointing, bowing, and nodding without training over the first 15 trials. Three dogs responded immediately to head turning, while the others learned to respond, and their performance increased during the trials. The dogs did not learn to respond to the glancing cue without training, but four of the six dogs learned to respond to this cue during the experiment. A second experimenter subsequently tested this second group to see if their response to the cues was independent of the person giving them.

Miklősi concluded that the dogs in both groups make use of physical cues. Dr. Miklősi argues that the dogs are not simply forming an association between a cue and the place of a reward, but that there is actual communication between the dog and human based

**Figure 3.5** Humans and dogs can communicate with one another in a variety of ways.

on earlier communicatory interactions: the dogs learn the meaning of the cue. The second group of dogs, having lived with humans for longer, had already learned much of this subtle communication, even without formal training.

## Glancing Cues

In most canids, the eyes play an important part in communication; however, the duration of eye contact might be crucial, as was noticed by Dr. M.W. Fox.[4] Dominant members of the pack use wide-open eyes during antagonistic stare-downs with low-ranking individuals. Behavioral observations suggest that enduring a direct stare from a human can either evoke submissive behavior in a subordinate dog or provoke an attack because the dog feels threatened in her home territory. Eye contact of shorter duration can lead dogs to initiate playtime. At the beginning of Dr. Miklősi's eyes-only trials, extended duration of eye contact or exaggerated gestures (i.e., small changes in the size of the signaling eye) might have been misinterpreted by some of the dogs as aggressive behavior. It should also be noted that in Miklősi's study, the human supplying the gestures was a not the dogs' owner but rather a familiar person. The dogs' general reluctance to respond to glancing cues could not be explained by attentional or motivational factors or by their inability to learn in the environment provided by the experiment. Therefore, in a 2001 experiment at the same laboratory in Hungary, the glancing cue was tested more extensively by Dr. Krisztina Soproni and her colleagues.[5]

Soproni wished to find out how the dogs (trained to respond to pointing) would react in three situations, where the researcher:

1. gestured at a target with both eyes and head
2. turned the head toward the target and kept the eyes focused above the target
3. kept the head still and only gestured at the target with the eyes

**Figure 3.6** By displaying minor body movements, the handler may unintentionally encourage and influence his or her dog while investigating a track.

Several trials with these three cues made up a "pointing" training session. Each cue was presented eight times to 14 dogs. The dogs responded to the head and eyes cue enough that their responses could not have been random, but they reacted randomly to the head-only or eyes-only cues. Next, the responses displayed during the first three sessions were compared with those from the last three sessions. There was no difference in the head-and-eyes cue or the head-only cue. However, it was found that the dogs avoided the eyes-only cue during the first three sessions, but they increasingly followed it during the second three sessions. It was argued that the dogs in the beginning perhaps misinterpreted the eyes-only cue since prolonged eye contact (staring) within canid communication is used by dominant individuals. Despite this, the dogs learned the cue's correct meaning quickly, even though they only received the cue eight times. This finding stresses the importance of eyes as a method for communication among dogs.

## Human Pointing Gestures

In 2002, Soproni and her colleagues deepened their research by testing the dog's responsiveness to human pointing gestures.[6] In the test, the dogs could find food pellets at a place indicated by humans. Six male and three female dogs aged two to seven years took part in the test. Except for three dogs, all of them had lived with the same human families since they were puppies; the others joined their current families as adults. One year earlier, four of these dogs had participated in experiments conducted by the same group of scientists, which involved pointing and gazing, but the dogs were naïve with respect to all experimental pointing gestures used in the 2002 experiment. The observations were carried out in each of the dogs' owners' apartments. Only the experimenter, the owner, and the dog were present during the training and testing. Soproni herself conducted all the trials.

Two bowls (brown plastic flowerpots, six inches [15 cm] in diameter, six inches high) were used to hide the food. Both bowls had double bottoms with one food pellet fixed under the separating panel. The bottom panels were covered with a cloth to prevent any noise while the food was placed in the bowls. Various brands of kibble were used for the reward.

During a pre-training session, Soproni stood 1.5 feet (0.5 m) behind the middle line between the two bowls, which were placed three feet (1 m) apart and were set on chairs. Six feet (2 m) in front of Soproni, the owner stood restraining his or her dog, which was facing the experimenter. Soproni tried to make eye contact with the dog and called her by name. When the dog was attentive, Soproni showed the dog a food pellet and placed it into one of the containers. Then the owner allowed the dog to approach the bowls and choose one of them. If the dog chose the baited bowl, she could eat the reward and was praised verbally by the owner. If the dog made an incorrect choice and went to the empty bowl, Soproni took the pellet from the other bowl and showed it to the dog. In this case, the dog would not get the food. This trial was repeated four times; the position of the food reward was counterbalanced. The pre-training was necessary to ensure the dogs knew that the bowls might contain food.

During the tests, the positions of the subjects were the same, but this time the dog was prevented from observing where the food was placed. Soproni took a piece of food in each hand and put one in each bowl simultaneously, but then she immediately removed one of the pellets. After the food was hidden, the owner stood behind the dog and made her sit facing Soproni. The owner was asked to let the dog go after the cue. Soproni made eye contact with the dog and gave the cue. She indicated the location of the food with various types of pointing gestures.

During the experiments, the dogs were presented with variations of the human pointing gesture: gestures with reversed direction of movement, cross-pointing, and different arm extensions. During *elbow cross-pointing* trials, Soproni stood in the middle line of the two bowls and pointed to the baited bowl with her contralateral hand in front of her body. She raised her arm in such a way that her extended index finger was at the middle line of her body, and her elbow protruded toward the empty bowl. In *far elbow cross-pointing* trials, Soproni stood next to the empty bowl (away from the baited bowl), and she indicated the food location from that position with her contralateral hand crossed in front of her body. In *pointing* trials, she stood at the middle line and pointed toward the baited bowl with extended arm and index finger. After signaling, she lowered her arm to the starting position beside her body. In *far pointing* trials, Soproni pointed to the baited bowl with her closer hand. In some trials, she used a stick as a pointer.

Dogs performed at an above-dumb-luck level if they could see the hand (and index finger) protruding from the contour of Soproni's body. If they could not see the index finger or hand sticking out, however, the dogs could still try to interpret Soproni's body position, such as the direction she faced. The direction of movement of the pointing arm did not influence the dogs' performance. In the end, the dogs were able to interpret and respond to relatively novel pointing gestures, and they were able to comprehend the referential nature of human pointing to some extent.

## The Detour Test

Péter Pongrácz and his colleagues from the Department of Ethology at the University of Budapest (Hungary) examined social learning in dogs: the effect of a human demonstrator on the performance of dogs in a detour task.[7] They recorded the behavior of dogs in detour tests, in which an object (a favorite toy) or food was placed behind a V-shaped fence. Dogs were able to master this task; however, they did it more easily when they started from

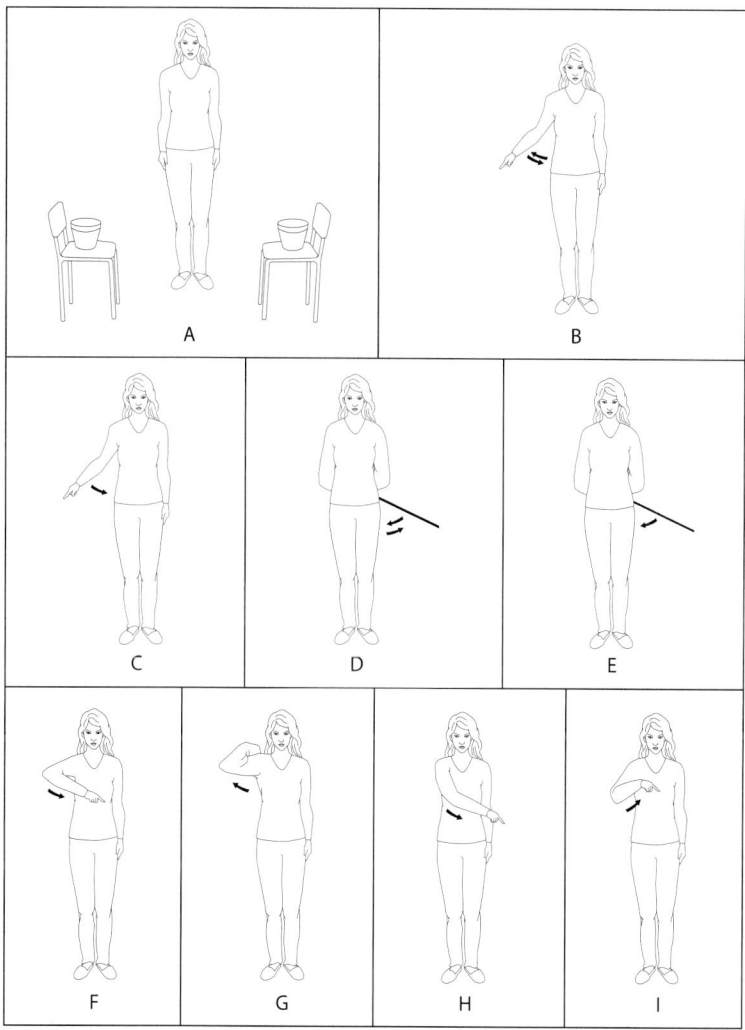

**Figure 3.7** Different pointing gestures Soproni used in her 2002 experiment.
A: The experimental setting.
B: Pointing and far pointing.
C: Reverse pointing.
D: Stick pointing.
E: Reverse stick pointing.
F: Elbow cross-pointing and far elbow cross-pointing.
G: Elbow pointing.
H: Long cross-pointing.
I: Short cross-pointing.

within the fence with the object placed outside. Repeated detours starting from within the fence did not help the dogs obtain the object more quickly if in a subsequent trial they started outside the fence with the object placed inside it.

While six trials were not enough for these dogs to show significant improvement on their own in detouring the fence from outside, when a human demonstrated this type of detour, the dogs' performance improved significantly over the course of two or three trials. Owners and strangers were equally effective as detour demonstrators. The experiments show that dogs are able to rely on information provided by human action when confronted with a new task. While they would not copy the exact path of the human demonstrator, they easily adopted the detour behavior shown by humans in order to reach their goal.

## The Importance of Working "Blind"

All of these experiments are important because they illustrate how well dogs can learn to "read" us. The case of Clever Hans demonstrates the extent to which an animal is able to observe and respond to subtle human gestures. But since this famous stallion performed his "tricks," much knowledge about the use of human-provided cues by animals has become lost to dog handlers, even professionals, leading to many faults in training as well as in serious practice.

It is widely believed that the dog's success in becoming "man's best friend" was due to the dog's ability to adapt to human behavior and social organization. Humans continuously and unconsciously use gestures in their communicative interactions, and dogs seem to be highly responsive to these cues.

Dogs are able to recognize human gestures—pointing, bowing, nodding, head turning, and glancing—as cues for finding hidden objects. Dogs are also able to generalize, recognizing that one person—the owner—can perform the same gestures as another familiar person (the instructor, for example).

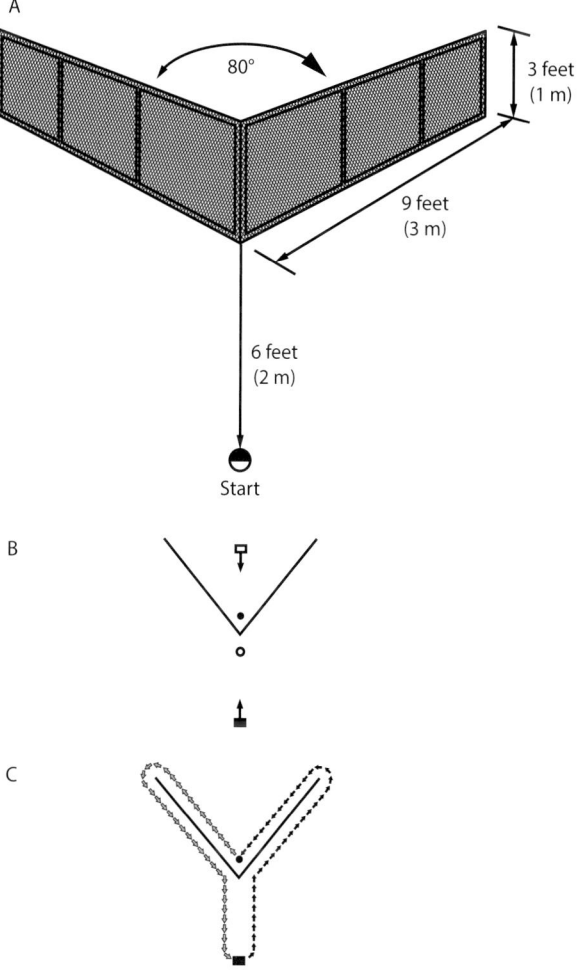

**Figure 3.8** Drawing of the V-shaped fence used in the experiments of Pongrácz and colleagues in 2001.

A: The steel-framed, wire-mesh fence was fixed into the soil by protruding pegs. The starting point for the Inward Detour group is indicated.

B: A sketch from above of the position of the starting point (black and white squares) and the position of the target (black and white circles). Black is the Inward Detour group; white is the Outward Detour group.

C: A sketch from above of a possible demonstration route; the other demonstration route is the reverse of the one presented. The human demonstrator carried the object to the inside intersection angle of the fence (black arrows) put it down, and left the fence (white arrows).

**Figure 3.9** To avoid influencing the dog, handlers should not know the position of the matching odor in a lineup or the hiding place in a search exercise. In fact, it is best that no one near the dog has this knowledge, as anyone could unconsciously cue the dog.

During training, we want dogs to respond to the relevant cues. So when searching for an odor, the only cue must be the odor. We have observed many handlers with their dogs, and sometimes the unconscious cues they provide are obvious. We have seen working dogs hovering over each odor in scent-identification lineups, carefully watching their handlers. A minimal movement is enough for them to then respond to that odor. We have also seen this behavior in training detector dogs—for instance, if the dog enters the hiding place where she is supposed to find something and the handler or other people stop talking or breathing, or the handler makes a small step forward, the dog will notice and respond to these cues.

How can we prevent ourselves from cueing our dogs, then, if they can pick up on and respond to such minimal signals as just glancing at the matching odor in the scent lineup or the hiding place? The answer is obvious: work "blind." Do not know the position of the matching odor or the hiding place and, preferably, have no one close by who knows it either, since that person may also unconsciously cue the dog. Such measures will enormously increase the searching dog's independent, successful performance.

# 4

# Tracking Dogs in Crime Investigation

In 1981, John Preston, a former Pennsylvania highway patrol trooper, and his dog Harass II followed an eight-day-old track over Highway 1A through the busy town of Titusville, Florida. The track ended at the house of William Dillon. Preston and Harass II later conducted a "paper lineup" that allegedly linked Dillon to a T-shirt found at the crime scene: Preston allowed his dog to sniff the T-shirt and then a series of pieces of paper, including one Dillon had touched. Preston said the dog selected Dillon's paper, and Dillon was arrested and charged with murder. After a five-day trial, in August 1981, William Dillon was convicted of the first-degree murder of James Dvorak and sentenced to life in prison.

## Tracking Dogs throughout History

The presence of dogs in protection services goes back a long way. As long as we have documented history, the dog has been companion to and guardian of the people protecting the peace—first as faithful comrade of the old-time night watchman with his horn and his halberd, and now as the service dog in the police, military, and intelligence services.

We can find traces of tracking dogs in the service of forensic investigation quite a long way back in history. Even the ancient

Greeks were well acquainted with the use of dogs for such tracking work. An ancient papyrus published in 1912 includes a fragment of a satyr play by Sophocles (496–406 BCE) called *Ichneutae* (*The Trackers*).[1] This somewhat risqué burlesque describes the well-known myth of the infant Hermes's theft of Apollo's cattle. Sophocles describes how satyrs, masquerading as herding dogs, pursue the track of the stolen herd and robber.

In the time of the Roman empire, Plinius (also known as Pliny the Elder) (23–79 CE) described in his *Naturalis Historia* (*The Natural History*) six categories of dogs: *villatici* (home or guard dogs), *pastorales pecuarii* (shepherd dogs), *venatici* (hunting dogs), *pugnaces* and *bellicosi* (fighting or war dogs), *pedibus celeres* (sighthounds), and *nares sagaces* (tracker dogs).

Much later, in the late Middle Ages, Heinrich Mynsinger wrote and published *The Book of Hawks, Goshawks, Sparrowhawks,*

**Figure 4.1** From the time of Pliny the Elder (79 CE), a Roman mosaic floor in the entrance of a house in Pompeii, including a *villaticus* with the well-known warning *cave canem* (Beware of Dog).

**Figure 4.2**
Woodcut from Mynsinger's 1473 text: "The dogs were also trained to track the trail of a thief…"

*Horses, and Dogs* (1473). The author based his work on old sources and speaks of regular police-dog training, which involved training the dog to stand up against a man clothed "in a stout coat of skins lest the dog should bite him during his education."[2] The dogs were also trained to track the trail of a thief, much in the same way that bird dogs (retrievers) are taught to search for partridge and quail. Mynsinger describes how a Dr. Meurer wrote about the tracking work of dogs and their training in 1460, basing his views of this on English standards.

M. Siber also wrote about the work of tracking dogs in a book published in 1899. Siber relates how people he met in South Africa used dogs to track the "spoor" of men and that, according to E. von Weber, "they often go out and bring back their runaway lady-loves with the help of dogs."[3]

Skipping ahead to 1923, Captain Max von Stephanitz refers to the memoir of painter W. von Kügelgen of Dresden (1772–1820), *An Old Man's Reminiscences of His Youth*. Kügelgen includes a story about how police dogs were used to search for his father, who was found murdered. Captain von Stephanitz writes:

> I wish to emphasize that it was the shepherd dog that inaugurated the police-dog movement and that it is he who is the moving spirit in it today. Our shepherd dog is a born police dog, for when he is with the flocks and the herds he is also

a "policeman." He maintains law and order, looks after the safety of his charges, punishes delinquents, and turns back trespassers. His development in the past from the dog of the Bronze Age to the Hovawart, a sheep and cattle dog, fostered and strengthened those very characteristics and inclinations that would make him the police dog par excellence: that is, joy in work, devotion to duty, loyalty to his master, mistrust and sharp awareness of strangers and unusual things, docility and obedience, teachability and quickness to understand, as well as immunity to weather, uncommonly acute senses, and an uncanny gift for retrieving and seeking.[4]

## Night Watchmen

In a series published in 1925, Belgian author Louis Huyghebaert expressed the general view that the shepherd dog was trusted from the beginning to take on the role of police dog. He wrote, "It is not easy to determine the precise time the dog started work in this role. An old document illustrating a dog in this role is an early 17th century woodcut. This woodcut shows a night watchman on duty, accompanied by a dog, in the Belgian town of Antwerp. The city archives mention that the first night watchman in Antwerp was chartered in 1597, and by 1627 there were 32 men on duty."[5] It is conceivable that protection dogs accompanied these night watchmen.

When we take a look at the woodcut, we see that these early police dogs were just as apt to bite as they are nowadays: the dog is helping his master by boldly biting the leg of the villain. The night watchman's weapons, in the foreground, show us that these men performed a serious task. The halberd and the long saber were used to bring felons to the lockup, and in the background of the woodcut, the night watchman's colleagues can be seen doing just that. Together with these weapons, the night watchmen made great use of their police dogs, as can be seen in a print from 1786, bearing the words "New Year's greetings from the night watchmen of the Belgian Town of Leuven."[6]

**Figure 4.3** Night Watchman of the Belgian Town Antwerp Accompanied by a Police Dog. Woodcut from the early 17th century.

**Figure 4.4** "New Year's greetings from the night watchmen of the Belgian town of Leuven." Woodcut from 1786.

## Police Tracking Dogs

After the French Revolution, at the beginning of the Reign of Terror in 1793, the use of police dogs in Belgium was abolished. The human rights declaration by the new French regime included a ban on dogs attacking people. This ban may have been prompted by police dogs having become too sharp and aggressive for public acceptance. After the abolition of police dogs in Belgium, more than a century passed before public administration resumed the use of dogs in police service.

Around 1890, dog enthusiasts near the Belgian city of Malines started to systematically train their Malinois, the short-haired Belgian shepherd dog, for protection and tracking work. Louis Huyghebaert, in particular, encouraged the training of the dogs in nose work. In an article from that time we read:

> While we walked together along the canal, Mr. Huyghebaert gave me his wallet, and during a moment when his dog Tom was not watching, I threw the wallet in the brushwood about

**Figure 4.5** Police-dog demonstration in Belgium, 1899.

three meters from the road. After walking on for a longer distance, Tom's master began to search his pockets and gesticulating as if he had lost something. Immediately the dog went back to the place where we had briefly paused and came back without having found anything. Seeing his master still inspecting his pockets, he ran back again, first tracking and then searching with his nose in the air. Soon he came back with a triumphant look in his eyes and the wallet in his mouth.[7]

Finally, it was in the Belgian town of Ghent that Superintendent Van Wezemael introduced three police dogs in March 1899. At the end of the same year, there were 10 dogs and by 1910, more than 30. All these dogs were Belgian shepherds, and most of them were of the Groenendael (a black, long-haired Belgian shepherd) and Malinois varieties. They were trained both for protection and nose work.

## Brilliant Dog Detectives in the Media

The use of these police dogs was such a success that soon many other Belgian towns, and even countries abroad, began to train and employ dogs in the police service. Numerous newspaper articles (especially in English and French) praised the dogs and caused such a demand for shepherds that many Groenendael crossbreeds (there were too few Groenendael dogs to meet the demand) and Malinois were exported to England, France, Germany, Russia, Argentina, and the United States. In most of these countries, police-dog training societies were founded.

Right from the start, police dogs captured the interest of journalists and the general public in these countries. This interest increased significantly when the dogs began to work as "detectives," investigating criminal cases. The value of the police dog was fully recognized when the first successes in solving homicides were recorded; from that moment on, the dogs became very popular. The first criminal investigations by dogs at the beginning of the 20th century caused quite a stir all over the world. The police-dog movement, at that time still in its infancy, began to grow.

It is interesting to read the German reports from that time, which include unbelievable (or at least incredible) tracking results. In several cases, after having followed a track, the dogs are reported to have performed suspect identification in scent lineups. A list of cases appears below; these stories are taken from Friedo Schmidt's book on police dog successes, published in 1911:

- In 1910, police dog Bolko of the Berlin police worked out a seven-day-old track and not only marked the place where the body of a murdered teacher was found near

**Figure 4.6** A German policeman with his dog in about 1910.

the river, but also tracked for two hours to a pub in the next village, where he barked at a chair the teacher had been sitting on. Based on this, a man who was seen with the teacher in the pub was arrested. The teacher had been killed because he was slated to make a statement in court against the suspect.[8]

- On April 4, 1910, police dog Harras I of the Cottbus police worked out a two-day-old track after getting odor from a matchbox found near the location of a fire. He followed a track approximately 900 yards (800 m) to an 11-year-old boy who caused the fire.[9]

- Despite a strong sidewind, the 18-hour-old, over 1 mile-long (3 km-long) track of an arsonist was worked out by police dog Wolf v.d. Treue in 1910, leading to the suspect's house.[10]
- In Flehingen near Bretten, during the night of October 20, 1906, a burglary took place in a post office, during which a person was seriously injured. The next day a suspect was arrested, but he denied involvement. On October 24, the German shepherd dog Luchs v. Frankfurt was brought to the crime scene. There the dog was given time to take in the odor of the crime scene and that of a pair of the suspect's socks, which were brought in.

  Then the dog tracked with his nose deep to the ground surface, first around the village and after that on the railway dam to the village of Bretten. Shortly before Bretten, the dog lost the track but found it again immediately after the village on the road to Dühren-Enzberg and worked out the track until Enzberg. The distance he tracked was over 17 miles (28 km), including the backtracking the dog sometimes did while tracking. The dog and handler stayed over in Enzberg, the residence of the suspect, and the next day Luchs tracked directly to the suspect's house. After the door was opened, the dog walked up the stairs to an attic room. Between two cupboards was a bag the dog barked at and tried to retrieve. After some time, the suspect's wife admitted that the bag belonged to the suspect. Nothing suspicious was found in the bag. After being confronted with the dog's work, the suspect admitted to having been in the post office, but he denied having been the burglar.

  Luchs failed to find the knife by which the suspect had injured the person. On the long way home, the suspect had enough time to dispose of it in such a way that it was untraceable, even for the dog's nose. If Luchs had worked out the track earlier, and not after four days, for sure it would have been possible for him to find this piece of evidence.[11]

In all or most of these stories, the handler had foreknowledge of the suspect, so results of the investigations are clearly questionable.

**Figure 4.7**
Successful tracking
to the suspect's
house.

## OTHER MIRACULOUS STORIES

Early police-dog literature often mentions similar, miraculous stories to those reported by Schmidt above. Most of the trainers, together with the journalists writing the accounts, speak in exaggerated terms about the results dogs were able to achieve. Within police and judicial circles, police-dog work was wholeheartedly trusted, and the clues provided by the dogs were accepted as solid evidence. Based on what we know today, however, these results were likely influenced by the handler or the "most likely" suspect.

- In 1906, to clear up a murder case, Inspector Bussenius from Braunschweig was called to the city of Mannheim with his dogs, Harras and Max. Several times, the dogs picked Becker, a furniture maker, out of a group of people. Becker was already suspected of this murder, and soon after the dogs indicated him, he admitted his guilt.[12]

- On December 24, 1908, the sex murder of a 10-year-old boy took place in the woods surrounding the town of Giessen. Despite his denial of involvement, the cobbler apprentice, Reif, was arrested for the crime. To establish conclusive proof of the suspect's guilt, the police dog Greif von Wetzlar, together with his handler Police Sergeant Jacob, tried to follow the track on December 27, in the afternoon. Greif was given the clothes from the child for scent since the murderer undoubtedly handled the clothes. The dog searched from the crime scene out, along a 2-mile (3.5-km) track, even though at least 72 hours had elapsed since the murder. To make matters worse, the ground was frozen stiff and a biting wind was blowing. Darkness stopped the dog's efforts that day.

The next day, the public prosecutor ordered several groups of people to be placed along the track established the previous day. Among them was the suspect Reif. After Greif was once again presented the scent on the clothes, he picked up on the same track and followed it until he came to the lineup of people. The dog sniffed briefly at the first two people, but when he came to the third, Reif, he sniffed him, barked, then lunged at Reif's chest so violently that they could hardly pull him away. After some time, Reif confessed to the murder.[13]

- In October 1909, Police Sergeant Jacob and Greif von Wetzlar solved another homicide case by picking up a trail that was several days old and which led through the whole town right into a room on the first floor of a restaurant/inn.[14]
- On Sunday, October 17, 1909, the forester Firnkes was stabbed and killed in a field near the village of Bruchsal; his body was found on Monday. Before the police arrived, the body and the crime scene had been examined by many people, and all traces of evidence and tracks were destroyed. On the evening of the 19th, the prosecutor contacted the police-dog unit in the nearby town of Weinheim and asked them to come to the crime scene.

So on October 20, three police dogs from Weinheim arrived in Bruchsal. That morning, gendarmes had arrested a person called Feuerstein. Feuerstein was known as a poacher, and he was suspected because he had been seen coming out of the fields that Sunday. Of course, Feuerstein denied everything. He was told to put on the clothes he had worn that Sunday. Subsequently he was lined up with 15 other people, 50 steps away from where the body still lay. The police dogs, all German shepherds, were separated. First a male, Melac, was brought to smell the body still lying at the crime scene. He was then led to the lineup. Melac quickly began to bark at Feuerstein, upon whose trousers stains were found that could have been washed-out blood. The police dog Pia also barked at Feuerstein when put through the same routine. The test had to be stopped here, because the body had to be brought to the town hall for an autopsy. In the yard of the town hall, however, Irma von Flügelrade sniffed the clothes of the murdered forester. Feuerstein was again placed in a line among other people, and Irma also barked at him. He was arrested after that on suspicion of murder, and soon after he confessed.[15]

- On the morning of November 20, 1909, near the town of Westpriegnitz at the Dallmin estate, which belonged to former minister of agriculture, His Excellency Otto von Podbielski, a nine-year-old girl was lured from the street into a pine forest and killed. The child was found that evening. The next day two policemen with their German shepherd dogs, Prinz von Mühlenberg and Bolko von Klostermansfeld, went to Dallmin. In the meantime, an attempt to pick up a track had already been tried with an Airedale terrier police dog from Havelberg, and the servants of the manor had carried out a search, all without result.

At the crime scene, where the body still lay, Prinz picked up scent from the child's clothes. Due to the onset of darkness, his handler worked with him on a long leash. With it snowing continuously, Prinz first tracked through the woods, then in the direction of the estate coach house. When they reached this house, the snow was so deep that Prinz could no longer follow the track.

The search for the murderer then concentrated on the people at the estate. One of them, a laborer with scratches on his face, was taken into custody. The gardener's helper, Pöhling, was also suspected, although he was thought to be innocent by the father of the murdered child as well as the examining magistrate. Both suspects stubbornly denied their involvement. Pöhling was placed in a line with other estate servants. Prinz sniffed at the pinafore of the child, since in the opinion of his handler this item of clothing would have the strongest odor of the perpetrator since it was a sexually motivated murder. After that, the dog searched around in the room, coming up to the line and smelling several people without making a sign. But after sniffing Pöhling, he immediately started barking and clearly made a signal by looking alternatively at his handler and at Pöhling. Suddenly, as if Prinz feared his signal might be misunderstood, he bit Pöhling on the leg. Pöhling again protested his innocence and explained that the dog only came to him because during the search for the lost child he had taken the body under the arm and lifted it up. Pöhling was told the dog had only sniffed at the lower part of the pinafore, which meant that he, Pöhling, must have also touched that area.

After that, Pöhling made a detailed confession, also saying that he stabbed the child in the neck with a pocketknife that he had thrown into a nearby thicket. Pöhling recounted that he had read a lot about police dogs and thought he was protecting himself by making his way back in a loop through the water and over a wire fence, hoping to erase his track in this way. The next day, November 22, the other dog, Bolko, took the scent from the hands of the murderer in the vicinity of the crime scene, and after a short time discovered the murderer's knife under a pine tree.[16]

- In the German town of Münden, during the night of February 1, 1910, several windowpanes in the house of an industrialist were broken. Twelve hours later, Police Sergeant Hattenbach from Hannover arrived with his German shepherd Afra von Gahrenberg. Afra picked up the scent from one of the stones that was thrown into the room. She searched for the scent of the perpetrator, leading the team over 660 feet (200 m) to a workman's house, where she barked at the door of a man named Sievert. The man was not home and was at work in a leather factory. Sergeant Hattenbach went there with Afra. He gave her the scent of the stone once again and sent her to search. There were 36 workers in the factory. Afra sniffed every man and, in spite of the acrid odor of tanning chemicals and leather, she soon was barking at Sievert. And even though the man denied involvement, he later paid for the windowpanes voluntary.[17]

- On Monday, January 9, 1911, a thief crept into the estate of a brewery owner called Dirigl in the German town of Vilsiburg. He was interrupted by a stable boy while he was putting oats into a sack, but he escaped, leaving the sack and one carpet slipper. The stable boy was not sure if he had recognized the thief, but thought it might be Dionys Riemer.

  On Monday, January 23, a fortnight later, the police dog Varus von Altfeld and his handler were ordered to go to Vilsiburg to find out if the lost slipper belonged to the suspected Mr. Riemer or not. Because Riemer was not home, a jacket that belonged to him was laid down behind his house. Varus picked up the scent from the slipper in front of the house. The dog barked at the jacket and also at a broom lying in a barn. Inquiry revealed that Mr. Riemer had recently brought this broom home.

  When Riemer returned home, the dog immediately attacked him. Hereupon the suspect was placed among other people, and Varus again picked up the scent from the slipper. Each time he was asked to find Riemer in the lineup, Varus attacked Riemer, who was sentenced to three months in prison on February 7, on the basis of the full conviction of the dog and other circumstantial evidence, and in spite of continued stubborn denial.[18]

- For years, a court secretary in the town of Dieuze was pestered by the worst type of anonymous letters. After hearing about the incredible results of the police dogs, he consulted Frontier Inspector Obst, who advised him to get some property of the people who might be writing the letters. These objects were hidden in various places.

**Figure 4.8** The suspect's boot was found as evidence.

Inspector Obst let his German shepherd dog Roland von Martinsberg pick up scent from the most recent of the anonymous letters. This nine-day-old letter had been sent to the police department in Strassburg. From there it was brought to the court in Dieuze and handed over to the victimized secretary, so it had passed through several hands. After Roland picked up the scent on this letter, he was sent to search. During several searches he always fetched property belonging to a Mrs. Zimmerman. The dog was then allowed to sniff Mrs. Zimmerman's hat, which he matched to the letter. Although the suspect denied it, the court convicted her.[19]

## Bold Dog Handlers

Beginning in October 1909, the SV, the Verein für deutsche Schäferhunde (German Shepherd Dog Society), offered a 25-Mark reward to the dog handler for every homicide case successfully solved by a German shepherd dog. Over a period of 18 months, the SV paid this cash prize 18 times.

Friedo Schmidt wrote uncritically about this phenomenal success in his 1911 book: "In this way, rapidly, one case after the other was solved, so that we can now look back upon a considerable number of murder cases successfully settled by the work of German shepherd dogs. This success cannot only be attributed to the perfect aptitude of the dogs, but certainly also to our bold dog handlers."[20]

Schmidt was right to praise the "bold dog handlers," because many of the cases from that time verged on or were impossible to solve by dogs. Now, of course, we can say that many of these cases involved incorrect human interpretations resulting in putting pressure on the "most likely" suspect with barking or biting dogs and/or were cases "solved" by the handler influencing his dog. Let's take a closer look at these common errors in K9 investigations.

## Incorrect Human Interpretations

An event described by J. Hansmann in 1931 illustrates how easily a dog's track can be mistakenly interpreted by people:

> After a burglary, indistinct footprints were found in the vicinity of the house, at two different places about 330 feet (100 m) from each other. A police dog handler from Berlin started with his dog at one of these spots. The dog picked up a track leading to the railway station. There, it was said that an unknown, suspiciously behaving man with a backpack, who could be described exactly, traveled from this small station with the first morning train to Berlin.
>
> But the dog handler went back to the crime scene and brought his dog to the second place where indistinct footprints were found. The dog now followed a track about 1 mile (3 km) in another direction to a secluded garden house. In the garden, the dog stopped at a spot that had been recently dug up. Here the greater part of the spoil was found.[21]

This example certainly demonstrates the value of having a good police dog working in crime investigation, but it also shows us how easily we can make mistakes in explaining the dog's work. If the dog handler had stopped after the dog worked out the track leading to the railway, it would have been assumed that the man with the backpack was carrying the stolen material. This, of course, would not have led to the correct conclusion.

## Putting Pressure on the Suspect

A good example of putting pressure on the "most likely" suspect with barking or biting dogs appears in the memoirs of Amsterdam police officer Jacob Water around the time of World War I:

> The public prosecutor in Maastricht, a town in the south of the Netherlands, asked for the assistance of my police tracking dog Albert. In a settlement near the Belgian border three days before, a murdered woman was found, and the only *corpus delicti* found at the crime scene was a handkerchief. After walking several kilometers, Albert led us to a cottage situated near a small path in the woods. A woman opened the door, and Albert darted inside. Soon I heard him barking and found him standing on a bed. I saw someone hiding under the blankets and called Albert to me. Soon the head of a man appeared. I identified myself as a policeman and ordered him to put on his clothes and follow me.
>
> Driving back to Maastricht, the prosecutor started questioning, but the arrested man claimed to know nothing about the woman. "Are you sure we got the right man?" the prosecutor whispered in my ear. But I whispered back to him: "You will hear it out of his own mouth." Thereupon, I said to the man: "Well, if you really are innocent, I'll tell the dog he is wrong. But know this: you can't deceive this dog. If you are lying, I can't answer for the consequences." I said this knowing that for criminals, police dogs are somewhat mysterious and frightening. Then, I used a trick I taught to Albert: to attack if I gave him a certain sign. I said aloud to Albert, "Albert, boy, it seems you were wrong." And then I gave him the signal. Growling, Albert shot out at the man, who, startled, cried, "Keep that dog away! Yes, I did it, I will confess!" And so this murder case was unofficially solved before we were back in Maastricht.[22]

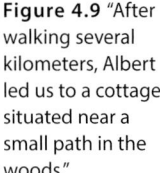

**Figure 4.9** "After walking several kilometers, Albert led us to a cottage situated near a small path in the woods."

In another case Officer Water includes in his memoirs, he again discusses this technique for forcing a confession:

> That morning I went with Albert to court. There I was told that two arrested men were suspected of a burglary, but they denied involvement. Two caps had been found at the crime scene that probably belonged to these men, although they denied this, too. Albert had to bring clarity to the case. I asked that a circle of policemen and other employees form up in the courtyard. Among them, the suspects were asked to stand, about four meters from each other. I let Albert take scent from one of the caps, and after having sniffed some other people, he stood barking in front of one of the suspects. After that, Albert took scent of the second cap, passed over the first suspect and went to the second one. Both arrested men insist on their innocence. "The dog probably made a mistake," they

said. "Well," I said, "in that case, I will tell him he was wrong." Just like the other time in the car, my trick brought the truth. Albert started growling and showed his teeth, after which the suspects suddenly remembered everything. They blamed each other, as usual, but they were put safely behind bars.[23]

## The Handler's Influence

As we've discussed, the Clever Hans Effect is one way you, the handler, can unknowingly influence the "achievements" of your tracking dog. Another way you may influence your dog is through the tracking leash, which provides contact between you and your dog. Your dog feels any movement of the leash when she is working. Whether or not you choose to work with your dog on leash depends on the dog's temperament and ability to handle pressure. When you alternate between keeping the leash loose and tight, you can control your dog's speed and eventually increase her willingness to work. By tightening the leash, you can stimulate your dog to move on even through difficult situations. But a dog that pulls on the leash may respond to a tightened leash by pulling even harder; this type of dog will go much too fast when the leash is slack. Most of the time, such dogs require you to correct them with commands. Conversely, you cannot hold the tracking leash too tightly on a somewhat unsure dog that tracks slowly because such a dog may feel the tight leash as a correction. In any case, too much pulling and adjusting of leash tension will upset the dog's concentration on the track, and she will make mistakes as a result.

Another big mistake is to pull the leash tight at certain moments in training sequences, such as during tracking training when the dog is searching for an article on the track, or when the dog must make a turn to stay on track. Some handlers will pull a sagging leash tight at these moments, or, if the leash is already taut, pull their dogs backward. If this type of correction continues throughout training, the dog will connect pulling tight or back with an article or a turn, and she will not search anymore. Instead, she will mimic tracking, head to the ground, waiting for her handler's signal. In this way, you, the handler, can also during a real mission easily lead your dog to the place you want to go.

The Clever Hans Effect was well known before World War I, especially in Germany, and the public was aware of the possibility of influencing animals in training. Despite this, the police and courts fully trusted the work and results of police tracking dogs. The value of police-dog input to crime investigations was highly overestimated.

## Critics of Tracking Dogs

Over time, dogs trained to follow a track were also used to identify individual people based on the odor of the track. There were some good results from this process, and soon faith in the tracking dogs' ability to point out guilty people became boundless. Soon enough, the dog's capacity was overrated. But, the pendulum started to swing back, and by 1913 the first critics of nose work made themselves heard.

### THE REMARKABLE NOSE OF A POLICE DOG

Public criticism of the uncritical attitude toward police-dog work produced priceless parodies, such as "The Remarkable Nose of a Police Dog," written by M. Soschtschenko in 1929:

> The fur coat belonging to Jeremje Bakkin, a merchant, was stolen. He was furious, because it was a very special fur. "That fur," he said, "was a peach. The money doesn't matter, but we have to find the thief and punish him," and he summoned a police dog to the scene. Soon a small man with a cap appeared in the village, accompanied by a medium-sized dog. It was a real cur, brown, with a pointed snout and an unpleasant expression.
>
> The man put his dog on the thief's track, said, "Psst," and let him go. The dog sniffed at the track and then looked at the spectators, local residents who had gathered to enjoy the spectacle. Suddenly the dog went to Grandma Fiokla who lived at Number 5 and sniffed at her skirt. Grandma tried to hide herself behind the others, but the dog grasped

her skirt. Suddenly she fell on her knees in front of the police officer. "Yes," she said, "I've been picked out and I don't deny it. I stole five buckets full of corn and a spirit lamp. Everything is in the bathroom. Take me to the police station." At that, all became silent. "And the fur?" they asked. "I know nothing of a fur," she answered. "But everything else is the truth. Take me to the station and punish me." Grandma was taken away.

The man put his dog back on the trail, said, "Psst," and let him go. The animal again looked round and walked up to neighbor Upradow, who turned pale, fell on his knees, and said, "Yes, it's true. Slap the cuffs on me. I collected the waterworks money and did not hand it over, but spent it for personal use." No wonder he was immediately captured by the local residents and taken away.

Meanwhile, the cur went to the resident of house Number 7 and grasped his trousers. The neighbor's face blanched with fear, and he fell on his knees. "I'm guilty," he exclaimed. "I tampered with my year of birth; otherwise, I would have had to go to war. Instead, I had an easy life, and I took advantage of it." Those present got excited and wondered what kind of a special dog this was.

Merchant Jeremje Bakkin blinked, took some money out of his pocket, and handed it to the policeman and said, "Take your dog away. For all I know that fur will never be found. Go to hell with your dog." But the mongrel was already there, standing in front of the merchant and smiling by waving his tail. With this, merchant Bakkin became agitated. He tried to leave, but the dog impeded his departure by going behind him and sniffing his shoes. The merchant shivered and turned pale. "He saw what I was up to," he said. "I'm an idiot and a thief," he continued. "The fur didn't even belong to me. I borrowed it from my brother and never gave it back."

Now all present began to run away, and the cur no longer took up the scent of the thief's track but instead grasped two or three of the nearest fleeing persons. All confessed. One of them had lost money entrusted to him at cards, the second had beaten his wife, and the third had uttered such curses that cannot be repeated here. The crowd was gone. Only the policeman and his cur were left. Then the dog went to the policeman and wagged his tail. The dog handler turned pale, fell on his knees in front of the dog, and said, "Just take me, then. It's true. I got three dollars for your upkeep and kept two of them for myself." And how it goes from here, I don't know, because I also got out of there![24]

The most outspoken criticism of dogs' tracking ability came from Berlin police-dog trainer (later a major) Konrad Most. During a trial, he voiced his doubt that police dogs could perfectly work out a five- to six-hour-old track. His statements caused commotion among handlers, and bitter words were spoken. To resolve the dispute, the Prussian Ministry of the Interior decided to implement a test of the best German police tracking dogs. The Berlin police started testing tracking dogs in 1913 and repeated these tests after World War I between 1920–1925 and 1927–1930. The results were poor: while following a track, the dogs were distracted by cross-tracks, and they lost the track altogether when it changed direction. During this same period of criticism, several training-instruction books and theories about how dogs track were published. Success stories and poor results alternated.

## Two Theories of Tracking

An interesting controversy about the way dogs follow a track illustrates the discussion that was taking place at this time of heightened awareness. There were two camps, each supporting a theory. According to one, the dog follows the individual scent that a person has left on the ground. According to the other, the dog follows the scent caused by the disturbance of the ground where a person has placed his or her feet.

Experiments conducted in 1887 by Romanes and in 1909 by Zell, as well as Blunk's theory from 1926, supported the first theory. In 1955, Neuhaus found that the threshold for butyric acid, a component of human sweat, is low enough for dogs to easily detect the amount left on the ground by an average footstep. However, the second theory was also widely supported. In 1905, Brough concluded that dogs were not able to follow a track once it had been crossed by another person's track. Directors of the German police-dog school in Grünheide were convinced that

Figure 4.10 In the 1930s, the Menzels used the dog's superb scenting ability to train dogs to follow an individual human scent on the track.

dogs could discriminate between people on the basis of scent but were unconvinced that this individual odor was in fact the guide dogs used when following a track.[25]

## TRAINING IS KEY

Experiments conducted by the Menzels (Dr. Rudolfina Menzel and her husband, Dr. Rudolf Menzel) in the 1930s and by B. Schmid in 1937 led to the conclusion that the key to how dogs work lies in the way they are trained. Training methods should therefore be closely adapted to the purpose for training, with sufficient controls built in to test what the dog has learned. With specific training, the Menzels and Schmid were able to train dogs to follow an individual human scent on the track.[26]

## Larry Harris, Dog Handler

In 1996, Superior Court Judge Tony Rackauckas in Orange County, California, shocked the district attorney's office when he overturned

**Figure 4.11** The Orange County judge stepped in on a verdict because of what he called a "canine catastrophe."

a jury's guilty verdict in the murder of an Irvine, California, woman. Larry Harris, a police-dog handler, had given testimony during the trial, claiming that his bloodhound Duchess had picked out 17-year-old high-school student Earl Henry Rhoney as the killer. Besides Harris's statement, there was no physical evidence that connected the suspect to the murder.

Rackauckas declared that Harris lacked credibility and overturned the jury's decision. Without Harris's testimony, the district attorney's case collapsed. Rhoney was freed after spending 42 months in jail. According to Rackauckas, it was "crystal clear" that Harris had dragged Duchess in Rhoney's direction during identification, that Harris had used a questionable homemade device to allegedly capture Rhoney's scent from the crime scene for the dog, and that the retired McDonnell Douglas engineer-turned-cop-aide was as "biased as any expert this court has ever seen."[27]

## Larry Harris, Dog Handler, II

Another victim of poor nose work (and bad police work) was James Ochoa, who spent 10 months in a maximum security cell at Theo Lacy Jail, one of Orange County's main jails, after he was found guilty of armed robbery. The only proof was the controversial evidence supplied by Larry Harris and his bloodhound Trace. Following is the case, as described by the Innocence Project.[28]

> At 12:30 a.m. on May 22, 2005, in Buena Park, California, two young Hispanic men were approached by another young Hispanic male, who pulled out a gun and demanded their wallets and the key to one victim's Volkswagen Jetta. The perpetrator wore a black baseball cap and a flannel shirt. He drove off in the victim's car with $600 from their wallets. The victims immediately called the police.[29]

As the responding officer heard the description of the robber from the victims, he thought of James Ochoa, who lived a few blocks away. Earlier that night, Ochoa and two of his friends had been sitting outside Ochoa's house. The officer had seen them there. He had searched them at the time, but found nothing illegal.

The officer pulled up a picture of James Ochoa and showed it to the victims. Both said that the man in the picture "looked like" the perpetrator.

At 1:00 a.m., police found the stolen car two blocks away from where it was stolen, only a little way from Ochoa's house. On the front seat of the car, police found a gray shirt and a black hat. Both victims told the police the clothing was not theirs, so it must have belonged to the thief. In addition, a black gun fell out from under the rear fender the moment the car was towed by police, and the victims said the gun was the sort of weapon used by the perpetrator.

The Innocence Project reports:

> At around 3:00 a.m., a bloodhound dog named "Trace" was brought to the scene. Over the course of one hour, Trace

allegedly followed the scent from a swab from the perpetrator's baseball cap to Ochoa's front door.

Ochoa was arrested and the two victims were brought to Ochoa's house around 6:00 a.m. Ochoa was standing on his front lawn, shirtless and in handcuffs. The victims identified him again.

They identified Ochoa a third time two months later in a live lineup.

The black baseball hat, gray shirt, gun, and the Jetta's steering wheel cover were all sent to the Orange County Crime Laboratory, where Ochoa was eliminated as a possible contributor to DNA on the evidence. More importantly, the major contributor on the baseball hat and on the gun grip exhibited the same unknown male profile. A CODIS database run could not identify the male. A latent fingerprint found on the Jetta's gearshift knob also did not match Ochoa or either victim.[30]

The *Orange County Weekly* reported that prosecutors attempted to pressure the crime-lab analyst who did the tests that exonerated Ochoa. According to the *Weekly*, a deputy district attorney had asked the analyst to change her report—indicating that James Ochoa could have been the perpetrator—before sharing it with Ochoa's defense attorneys, but she refused.

A judge threatened Ochoa with a sentence of 25 years to life in prison if a jury found him guilty, and against his attorney's advice, Ochoa accepted a plea bargain in December 2005 that led to a sentence of two years in prison.[31]

As R. Scott Moxley wrote in the *Orange County Weekly* in November 2005:

> The weakness of the case is only underscored by Harris's pivotal role in the arrest. Though police claim that Harris's bloodhound, Trace, ran directly to Ochoa's front door, the real story is far less incriminating. In truth, Trace twice ran by Ochoa's residence without noticing. According to a police report obtained by the *Weekly*, it wasn't until Harris pointed the dog back toward Ochoa's house that she allegedly ended her hunt there.

**Figure 4.12** Though police claimed that Harris's bloodhound, Trace, ran directly to Ochoa's front door, the real story was quite different.

"This was the only door she showed any interest in all evening," Harris wrote. "It was later confirmed that the subject that lived at that location was involved."[32]

But, as Moxley pointed out, there are several big problems with Harris's claims. First, the police logs show it took Trace 63 minutes to find Ochoa's house, even though Harris described the dog's scent tracking to Ochoa's residence as only about 50 yards (45 m). Second, the police were allegedly so satisfied the dog tracked a scent to Ochoa's front door that they let Harris and his dog leave without identifying Ochoa. Moxley continued, "Harris claims his dog's identification was solid but failed to note a breach of FBI guidance regarding search dogs: instead of keeping the stolen-car crime scene clean, police swarmed it. Those same officers later surrounded Ochoa's home, and were followed by Trace. It's conceivable, in other words, that Trace had done nothing more than follow the scents of officers she had first picked up around the stolen car."[33]

Furthermore, the claim that Trace ran directly to Ochoa's front door does not match other descriptions saying Harris's bloodhound ran by Ochoa's residence two times without noticing. A police report notes that Harris pointed Trace back toward Ochoa's house.

As Moxley scathingly wrote, "It's a catalog of sloppy police work, callous prosecutors, indifferent judges and a brazen contempt for exculpatory evidence. The story would be comical if the consequences weren't so dire."[34]

According to the Innocence Project, it was not until October 2006 that James Ochoa was exonerated when Jaymes T. McCollum entered the Los Angeles County Jail on carjacking charges. McCollum's DNA was entered into CODIS, and Pete Montez, a Buena Park police officer, noticed that McCollum's DNA matched the unknown male profile from Ochoa's case. McCollum confessed to the May 2005 carjacking when Montez confronted him. Montez told the Orange County DA, who filed a People's Petition for Immediate Habeas Corpus Relief on October 18, 2006. By the morning of October 20, 2006, Ochoa had been told he was leaving prison, but without a lawyer, Ochoa did not know about McCollum or that his sentence had been vacated. He got a ride back to Orange County in a DA vehicle, and officials bought him lunch and some clothes—not much compensation 16 months after being arrested for a crime he did not commit.[35]

### HANDLER'S SIGNALS

Larry Harris clearly led his dogs to the conclusions he wanted. Handler influence on dogs is still a problem, not only in K9 units, but also in the world of hobby tracking and investigation. Many dogs pass their tracking examinations after being led by their handler over the track. If professional search dogs get used to reacting to the slight signals of their handlers, the dogs will be unable to search independently, with sometimes life or death consequences.

**Figure 4.13** The results of tracking can be trusted only if the handler does not know the path of the track.

To avoid this problem, as soon as the dog knows how to track or search, she must work "blind." The handler cannot know the suspected course of the track or the hiding place—and anyone else who is present should also be ignorant of the direction of the track and the final destination.

Professor David Katz of Stockholm University emphatically points out that K9s and sports dogs will never reach a high level of tracking if we, the handlers, trainers, and instructors, do not understand the influence of the Clever Hans Effect and continue to fool ourselves and cheat our dogs: "Tracking only makes sense if the handler does not know the direction of the track."[36]

## John Preston, Dog Handler

Former Pennsylvania highway patrol trooper John Preston was introduced at the beginning of this chapter. His claims about his dog verged on the incredible, and in fact were impossible. Preston not only lied under oath about the training of his dogs, he also rigged many searches. Police and court reliance on Preston and his "proofs" wrecked many lives. William Dillon was not the only one who suffered because of the "evidence" provided by Preston and his dogs. Preston put at least 15 men behind bars and, in some cases, on Death Row.

In all the states where Preston appeared with his magic dog, he claimed to perform tracking feats that, frankly, are not even physically possible for a tracking dog, no matter how well trained or how talented. And Preston's dogs were not especially well trained. Preston traveled around the country, dropping in to work with police and then testifying about his dog's "finds." Although he was court-certified as an "expert," he was not, and neither his tracking evidence nor his testimony was reliable.

Preston did have his critics in the courts, such as Gilbert Goshorn, a former Brevard County judge, who went so far as to test one of Preston's dogs. Goshorn designed a test in 1984 to determine if the dog could do what Preston purported. Goshorn asked two lawyers to jog down separate paths. The following morning, the dog was given one lawyer's sweat-soaked shirt to see if the dog could follow the trail. The dog failed. Goshorn told Preston that

**Figure 4.14**
The problem was not with Preston's dogs—they were simply income- and glory-producing tools used by Preston for his ongoing self-promotion.

he would give him a second chance a day later, but the handler and his dog left town and never testified in Brevard again.

"It is my belief that the only way Preston could achieve the results he achieved in numerous other cases was having obtained information about the case before the scent tracking so that Preston could lead the dog to the suspect or evidence in question," Goshorn said his affidavit. "I believe that Preston was regularly retained to confirm the state's preconceived notions about a case."[37]

Prosecutors continued using Preston's services even after a 1983 federal investigation into Preston. This investigation said Preston routinely asked investigators for information about a case before using the dog and that he led his dog to supply wanted results.

Preston's cases were overturned in Arizona, where the state's highest court referred to him as a "charlatan," and Geraldo Rivera exposed the con on national television in 1984.

Titusville attorney and former Brevard prosecutor Sam Bardwell, who encountered Preston in a 1981 rape case, says then–State Attorney Doug Cheshire, as well as the Brevard sheriff's office and most law enforcement officers at the time, knew Preston was a charlatan. "I left the state attorney's office because I could not abide by the fabrication of evidence," Bardwell said. "Fabrication of evidence" is a serious charge, proven in Preston's case.[38]

Late in 2008, a relieved William Dillon left Florida's toughest prison after incarceration for 27 years for a murder he did not commit. DNA evidence excluded him from connection to a key piece of evidence. The discovery of this evidence made it clear that the "evidence" John Preston and his German shepherd Harass II produced against him in 1981 was entirely false. Unfortunately, such handler-led tracking and false testimony are not things of the past.

5

# Scent Research and Tracking Experiments

One of the biggest problems in scent work is that humans lack the sensitivity of the dog's nose and the dog lacks the human's interest in certain scents. Ordinarily a dog pays attention to completely different items than we humans do. A lot of things we do not pay attention to, or even turn up our noses at (sometimes literally, because they stink so much) are of great importance to dogs. It is best to be aware of these differences in observation between human and dog, so we can better understand the behavior of dogs during search work. Because of a difference in interest, our world and that of dogs looks different. This was described clearly by German Professor Dr. J. von Uexküll in 1934:

**The Human World**
A human and his dog walk together in a town. They pass a clothes shop and the human pauses to view the items on display. Then they pass a jeweler's, where rings and watches in the shop window catch the human's eyes. The pair then go by a bookstore, where the human stops to browse through books and magazines on an outdoor rack. The human pays less attention to the butcher shop next door and instead proceeds to walk around a corner into a park, up a staircase, and onto a terrace, where he sits on a chair and looks at the nice flowerbeds around him.

### The Dog World

The dog experiences the world totally differently when he goes out for this same walk. He passes the clothes shop; the things displayed there do not interest him. These only become of interest when his owner or another housemate has worn them and they have absorbed the person's body odor. The jewelry and books also do not interest him. Their display is nothing more than an unimportant mess of lines and surfaces imparting an uninteresting odor. The butcher shop says more to him. The odor of meat and sausages sparks his appetite, and the smell of waste makes him want to roll in it. And then there is the pillar on the street corner. How could his owner have almost passed it by? Every male dog that went by this stone has planted a more or less strong odor flag. The dog knows he must study these odor flags very seriously, and after he has added his scent, he can continue his walk. The staircase of the terrace is like walking up a hill, and he may not even notice that the slope is interrupted by stairs. The rail of the staircase is unimportant, but the cushions on the terrace chairs interest him. They are very soft. He likely notices nothing of the flowerbed's beauty—only when he spies a mouse darting under a leaf does he pay attention to the park.[1]

## Different Worlds

What the dog perceives is not coincidental to her environment but depends largely on her interests; her perception is active, not passive. Sensory impressions affect dogs when they have a biological meaning: that is, when objects play an obvious role in a dog's life, she will pay attention to them. For example, the odor of other dogs is important, as is the sound of a barking dog or the sight of a cat crossing the street.

The amount of attention a dog pays to a certain perception also depends on experience. A dog's reaction to the approach of a person or another animal she recognizes by odor or sound depends on what the dog knows of that person or other animal; her experience informs her perception and therefore her response. And through

training, the dog can be become interested in things that an un-
trained dog may not even notice.

## Prickle Thresholds

When looking at dogs' sensory capabilities, people have wondered
if canine senses are as strongly divided from one another as they
are in humans. In many situations, dogs do combine seeing and
smelling, and they likely possess a different "prickle threshold" for
sensory perceptions that naturally cooperate, as opposed to those
that are separately stimulated. It is illogical to suggest that tracking
dogs only use their noses and do not search with their eyes for soil
damage or changes in the terrain.

It is critical for trainers and handlers to understand the concept of the *prickle threshold*. Imagine that awareness lives in a
ground-floor room of a house, and that any sensory impression
approaching awareness, like a visitor to the house, first has to step
over the threshold of the house before awareness notices it. However, awareness may abide in a second-floor or third-floor room;
the higher the room, the higher the sensory impression must step
to attain the threshold of that room, and so the stronger the sensory prickle has to be to step over the threshold and penetrate
awareness.

The threshold value, in any given case, is the minimal prickle
strength needed to cross the threshold and penetrate awareness.
We can imagine the sensory impression crossing the threshold in
two ways: one, in a form just strong enough for awareness to notice
its existence; and two, so strong that we are not only aware of it,
but can observe certain qualities about it.

For example, a weak beam of light can be just strong enough
for the human eye to observe the clarity of the light without noticing anything else about it. We then would say that this beam of
light has passed the *absolute* prickle threshold. As the light slowly
becomes brighter, the eye will begin to observe the properties of

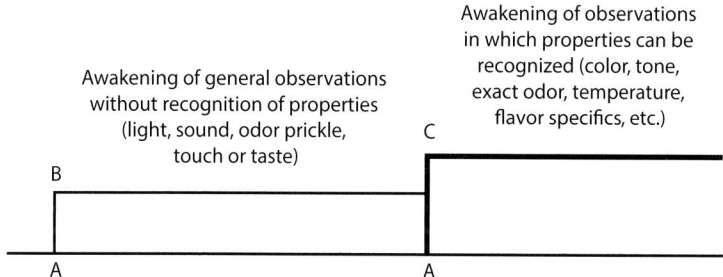

**Figure 5.1** Schematic representation of the absolute (A–B) and specific (A–C) prickle thresholds.

the light, such as its color. We then speak of passing the *specific* prickle threshold.

The same, of course, is true of the olfactory sense, a sense incredibly important to dogs. An odor (for instance on an old human track) can be just strong enough to be smelled by a tracking dog. But the odor may no longer be strong enough to give the dog particular information about it, such as the specific odor of the tracklayer. The strength of the track's odor would then be considered above the *absolute* but under the *specific* prickle threshold.

## Various Levels

The prickle threshold for various senses is not experienced uniformly throughout the animal world. Different creatures, even different creatures of the same species, have different prickle thresholds. For instance, some dogs will bark at any approaching stranger, while other dogs will let a stranger into the house without any fuss at all. Many factors influence the strength of a prickle threshold, such as health, way of life, reception, acquaintance, interest, hunger, training, or level of fatigue. For example, if we take good care of ourselves, we know that at different times we will react differently to prickles coming at us from the outside. Depending on circumstances, we say of ourselves that we are in a good or bad mood, irritated or nervous. Under the influence of these factors, our prickle threshold levels can change substantially.

It is similar with dogs. Anyone who has spent time observing dogs knows they also experience good or bad moods, which can alter their prickle thresholds in positive and negative ways. The dog's nose, its finest instrument, is particularly sensitive, especially when we demand high performance from it. Many factors can affect whether the absolute or specific prickle threshold for an odor is at a higher level than normal, to the point of an odor failing to cross the threshold altogether.

## Factors Affecting Sensory Perception

The problem with using a dog's nose for our detector and tracking work is not entirely a physiological one, so it is not a question of the capabilities of the nasal organ itself, but rather a psychological one, depending on the dog's intelligence and ability to learn, the attention of the dog, and her present prickle threshold.

Sensory perception is not a straightforward process but is instead a combination of different factors. In the first place, in order for the dog to make a sensory perception, she must have a fully functioning and well-built infrastructure (eyes, ears, nose, and so on). As well, from these organs there must be a functioning nerve connection to the related brain center. Each part of the system must be functioning properly in order for an accurate perception to be made. But to even notice things, there must be, for any given sense, a specific and sufficiently strong prickle, and the dog's attention must be directed toward this prickle. Only when all these factors are operating can the dog perceive.

### FATIGUE

The effects of fatigue can play a very important, sometimes even a deciding, role in perception. Tiredness can affect all stages of perception, from intake (for example, the nose) to processing and perception (in the brain). In the nose, for instance, the time it takes to expire breath must be long enough for the olfactory mucosa to recover and be ready for the next intake of breath. The same is true of the nerves, which have to be able to carry the prickle to the brain. Physical tiredness can show up in search work or tracking, particularly on longer tracks. So we certainly do not advise doing any tiring work with your dog just before tracking. For better results in tracking, as in every form of search work, it is best to start with a physically well-rested dog.

We sometimes see mental tiredness in dogs working out long and difficult tracks, especially when the odor is close to the prickle threshold, or even under it, so that the dog has to stumble a bit over the parts where there is no odor, and hence no prickle. A dog may also become mentally fatigued when she has to work continuously, for a long time, especially when it is very warm or if the dog is under pressure (from her handler, difficult surroundings, unusual amounts of travel, and so on). Under such circumstances, despite a normal effort, the dog will deliver poor results. Dogs express tiredness by having reduced attention to things they would normally be interested in. During tracking, for instance, a tired dog will slow down, lose interest in the track or search work, and be diverted by any little thing: she will catch flies, relieve herself, and so on. You can sometimes get your dog to overcome tiredness by directing her attention back to the track.

## Odor Summation

Philosopher Dr. Rudolfina Menzel and her husband, physician Dr. Rudolf Menzel, describe the important concept of *odor summation*. A prickle that is too weak by itself to be perceived (and is thus under the absolute threshold level) can become more noticeable if it is constantly and continuously picked up. Though separate, the weak prickles following each other will add up (summarize) and can become so strong together that they can cross the absolute and even the specific prickle threshold. Through accumulation, the individual, weak prickles become a sort of ladder, allowing a weak prickle, the last rung on the "ladder," to cross to a higher threshold.

It is like having a small pain, such as a headache. We normally do not discover such pain suddenly. Becoming aware of it is not a result of the pain becoming more severe over time, but because the pain prickles have added up and come slowly to our awareness.

Alternatively, picture being asleep when the alarm goes off. You are so deeply asleep that at first you do not notice the alarm. When sleeping, your prickle threshold is so high that even a loud, piercing tone cannot cross the threshold. The alarm continues to ring, so the noise summarizes into prickles that cross the absolute prickle threshold, allowing you to hear the noise in your sleep. Of course, you may not instantly recognize the noise as your morning alarm. It is not unusual to dream of fire alarms and sirens until the prickle manages to cross the specific prickle threshold, at which point you recognize the well-known tone (which most of us do not like so much) and awaken.

If you want to understand the tracking dog's work, it is important to first understand this summarizing effect and to employ it while training dogs. For instance, on older tracks, the amount of human odor in one footstep can be under the specific prickle threshold, not enough to be perceived by the dog. Only through the summation of the odor prickles, so over the course of a longer track, is it slowly possible for the tracking dog to perceive anything about the odor quality of the tracklayer. The summation of prickles does not require an uninterrupted sequence of weak prickles. But frequent repetition at certain intervals between prickles can strengthen weak prickles enormously. This is also the secret of advertising, namely that a one-time ad can go unnoticed because it doesn't grab our attention, but the same ad confronting us almost daily will work its way into our distracted brains. In the same way, a certain human odor can, by repetition, work its way into the dog's mind, so that he can clearly work out old, clean-scent tracks (tracks formed solely by human footsteps). The easiest way to train your dog to track, of course, is to ask her to work on your own track or that of a regular, known tracklayer.

## Systematic Training

One of the biggest mistakes handlers make in many general tracking or search-dog training sessions is to believe that their dogs know what humans expect of them right from the start. Some believe that their dogs will be instantly interested in any odor they want them to be interested in, and that the dogs will automatically concentrate on that odor. These handlers unconsciously think that getting a dog to track a scent is as simple as giving the dogs orders to sit or lie down. But the work of searching and tracking, unlike the simple command–response training required to get a dog to lie down, is the product of a longer, more systematic training method that has to go in two directions at once.

First, you, the handler, must bring the dog's attention to focus on sensory impressions the dog would never be interested in by herself. The second task is to train your dog to respond to keywords that can help bridge the gap between your needs and the dog's understanding.

The bond between dog and handler is never more visible than in search work. Here you cannot achieve anything through violence or pressure. Only a good understanding between you and your dog makes it possible to be successful. With search work, we must be willing to follow the dog in her world, and to recognize her superiority there.

**Figure 5.2** Search work allows humans to supplement our own sense organs with another creature's organs—to gain admittance to a world of odors that would otherwise be closed to us.

## Research on Canine Olfaction

To gain knowledge about the dog's smelling ability, people began researching canine olfaction more than a century ago. What followed were many thousands of tracks and numerous scent tests, including the pioneering research of Most, Brückner, Böttger, Hansmann, Belleville, and the Menzels, not to mention the many scent tests of Dr. Walter Neuhaus. All these successful experiments elucidated knowledge we now ponder while scent training our dogs. It is, however, a pity that so many present-day handlers, instructors, and even judges do not know about (or disregard) all the valuable and useful results that came of these important search-dog tests. Such knowledge would enormously increase the general quality of tracking, trailing, and detector dogs, both for sport and professional uses.

## THE FIRST TRACKING TESTS

In 1885, G.J. Romanes researched the ability of the dog to follow human footsteps.[2] In the important scientific journal *Nature*, he described in 1887 how his dog, a setter, could follow his track even though it was covered with the tracks of 11 other people. All his tests were done with his own dog, which had a strong bond to Romanes (and also had a good nose).

While his dog was held by a helper, Romanes (decked out in his hunting clothes) walked into the shooting grounds. He walked for about a mile, until he was out of sight of the helper, who then loosed the setter. The dog hurled himself with full enthusiasm and speed onto Romanes's track and very soon caught up with him. Even when Romanes rubbed his shoes with aniseed oil, giving the track a strong aniseed odor, the setter followed his track after only some hesitation.

In another test, Romanes placed 11 people in a line one behind the other and then positioned himself in front. He led this group forward thus, with each person's footstep placed in the footstep of the one who walked before him. After about 197 yards (180 m), Romanes turned right, keeping five helpers behind him, while the six others went to the left. His setter was brought to the shooting grounds and began to track. At the branch, the dog first walked on, then searched more intensively and located the correct track to the right. With that result, it was accepted that the dog was able to find and work out the track of his owner out of a mix of 12, and later on out of six, tracks.

However, the dog could not successfully work out the track of a strange person. He did not even want to work out the track of a gamekeeper he knew well. After that, Romanes decided to exchange his boots for those of a strange person and both he and the stranger laid tracks. The dog worked out the track laid by the stranger wearing Romanes's boots, but he did not pick up Romanes's track laid with the strange man's boots, even when he was encouraged to do so.

Romanes continued his tests and laid a track in socks he had worn for a while. The dog didn't pick up this track either, but when Romanes laid a track in bare feet, his dog worked it out, although slowly and with some hesitation. When his handler laid a track wearing new boots, the setter did not locate the track.

Romanes then glued brown paper onto the soles and sides of his old boots and laid a track. In the beginning, the setter did not pay much attention to the track, but that changed when he came to a place in the track where a piece of paper had been loosened from the heel of the boot. The dog recognized the track of his handler at this point and followed it cheerfully, although this little piece of paper was only a few square fractions of an inch.

Romanes concluded that his dog was not just working out his track but also that of his hunting boots; the setter was following a composite scent consisting of the leather of the boots and the odor of Romanes's feet. The dog could, however, very clearly distinguish the odor of his handler from that of the boots, as was proved by another experiment. For this one, Romanes walked about 55 yards (50 m) in his boots, then almost 328 yards (300 m) in his socks, and after that the same distance in his bare feet. His dog worked out the track until the end, and Romanes concluded that the dog, after first following the mix of scents, could not only recognize a single part of it, but could also follow that part. Despite all this intricate work, the setter never did succeed on strange tracks.

It is too bad that the results of these experiments were little known at the beginning of the 20th century by the police, who at that time fully trusted the tracking dog and accepted the dog's results as convincing evidence, even though it was often obtained by influence from the handler or the possible suspect.

## SYSTEMATIC RESEARCH

The first person to systematically research tracking dogs, and to publish on the subject in 1910, was Dr. Friedo Schmidt from

Stralsund, Germany.[3] He described how human odor substances immediately or soon after penetrating shoes made contact with the surface of the ground, forming a track that dogs could smell. In the same way, human odor substances penetrate gloves and are left behind on other articles that have been touched. He proved that trying to hide an individual human odor or to lay an "odorless track" with new shoes made tracking more difficult for the dog but did not make it impossible.

Schmidt also noted that if a dog were in poor physical condition—as a result of poor nutrition or extreme physical exertion—her ability to track could be negatively affected.

In spite of the clear results of his research, Schmidt pointed out that a successful track by a police dog must be seen only as an indication and not as evidence. This advice was not accorded sufficient weight later on, so that before and after World War I, there were intense discussions about the value of the police dog on the tracks of criminals. Therefore, the Prussian minister of the interior asked well-known police dog trainer Konrad Most for his advice about this matter.

## Most's Tracking Cross

Konrad Most had many police tracking dogs available for his research. After he proved that a dog could easily move over from one track to another, he investigated the cause and conditions under which a dog might follow the wrong track. His research concerned two questions:

- What is an odor track for a dog and which odors lead the dog?
- How long is it possible for a dog to follow track laid by a shod human?

After countless tests, Most developed a tracking scheme that became known as Most's Tracking Cross. One tracklayer walks

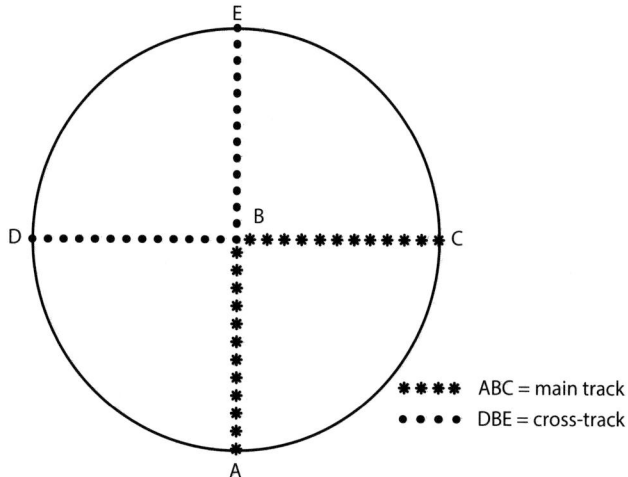

**Figure 5.3** Most's Tracking Cross. One of the most difficult tracking exercises for a dog is to follow track ABC. In many tests, dogs have tracked correctly from A to B, but at the cross-track may cross over to E.

from A to C, and another tracklayer from D to E; they meet at point B. The dog starts at A and is supposed to track to C, with DBE offering a tempting cross-track.

Because all the dogs Most tested arrived at B and then followed the track to E or made other mistakes, Most concluded in 1914 that dogs are not able to follow the individual human odor on a track; they are not "track-sure." He also concluded that dogs cannot recognize articles scented with the tracklayer's odor on the basis of the track's odor, and that dogs can only follow tracks that are no more than five hours old.

## REPEATING THE TESTS

When World War I broke out, Most had to stop his research on tracking dogs, but in 1920, Most repeated his earlier tests with the best tracking dogs of the time. The result was, as it was before, disappointing and proved that the tested dogs were not track-sure. When there were cross-tracks on strange terrain, the dogs always went astray.

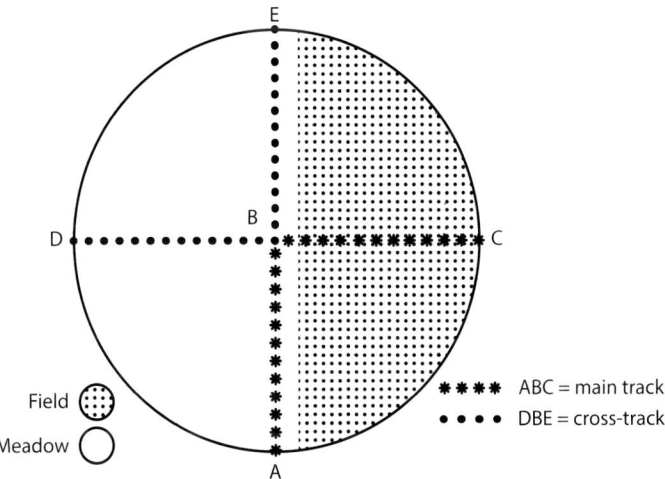

**Figure 5.4** Most's Tracking Cross with a change in terrain is very difficult for dogs to work out.

In another test, Most employed 13 trained dogs, one of them a gundog. The owners of these dogs were convinced their animals could recognize and follow the tracks of their handlers from among other tracks. The 52 tests showed 10 correct and 42 wrong results; no single dog did everything correctly, but only as often as could be expected in terms of probability. When presented with only a single strange track in the field, the dogs often followed the wrong track and did not find their handlers. There were cross-tracks in each of these tests, which presented serious difficulties. Most concluded that dogs are tempted more easily than humans, as they only focus on their senses and the direction of their attention at the moment, and they do not have a rational or critical consciousness.

With cross-tracks, the angle to the main track is important. If the turn is much less than 90° to the track, it is unlikely for the dog to go over to the cross-track. If the turn, however, is much more than 90°, forming an obtuse angle to the track, there is a greater chance that the dog will go over to the cross-track, especially when the cross-tracks are younger and so have more odor (which strongly attracts a dog).

One of the most difficult tasks for a tracking dog is to follow a track connected to a cross-track in the scheme of Most's Tracking Cross. It becomes still harder when there is also a change from one terrain to another, such as a change from a meadow of native plants into a cultivated field. The tests done with Most's Tracking Cross, even according to Konrad Most himself, are among the hardest exercises for a tracking dog.

## Controversy

The publication of Most's research led to much controversy because supporters of the use of police tracking dogs, such as criminologist Paul Böttger and veterinarian Dr. J. Hansmann from Berlin, felt the work of these dogs to be threatened. They knew they could prove in practice much better results than Most's tests showed.

In the opinion of Most, given the training techniques of that time, police tracking dogs only followed the scent of physical changes to the ground surface, namely the smell of sap from damaged plants and rotting bacteria. In his view, dogs were not track-reliable. On the other hand, German researchers Dr. J. Hansmann, Paul Böttger, and Dr. R. Blunk, along with the Menzels from Linz, Austria, continued to believe that tracking dogs followed human odor substances transferred to the ground.

## Extensive Experiments

Extensive tests followed: Konrad Most and Dr. G.H. Brückner, between 1927 and 1930, conducted as many as 1268 tracking tests. Between 1930 and 1935, Major R. Belleville conducted a total of 1458 tracks, with 4404 cross-tracks. Dr. J. Hansmann and Paul Böttger declared that, between 1925 and 1932, they tested "many thousands" of tracks in the German Police Dog School of Grünheide.[4]

Even after 1930, Konrad Most continued his experiments. He developed a cable-lift and a big wheel with wooden and porcelain shoes attached so he could lay tracks without human odor. He used the cable lift to pull a person on a float appliance close above the ground surface, without touching the ground.

## CONTROL TEST

The first of Most's cable-lift experiments employed four well-trained police tracking dogs. All dogs were first put to a control test, as described by Most: "A test person walked from A to B and from there back to A. The dog started to track at A. All dogs tracked from A to B, and then circled the end point without walking past the end of the track, as a lot of badly trained dogs do. At B the dogs were not called back, but they tracked back to A on their own."[5]

## AIR TRANSPORT

Next, tests were done to answer the question of whether or not "odor substances" from a person transported through the air would fall down to the ground, so that the dog could sense them. This was and still is supposed. In 1958, R.J. Clifford, and in 1972, W.G. Syrotuck, published the theory that flakes of skin fall from the human body and so form an important odor track for the dog. In the time of Konrad Most, it was thought that some kind of "odor substance" fell down from someone walking on stilts or riding a bicycle, a type of substance that floats in the air or lies on the ground.

The deciding test was worked out by Most as follows. A person walks the distance from A to B, where he or she sits on a plank on the float appliance and is transported farther while his or her feet are about 12 inches (30 cm) above the ground. Immediately after that, the dog is placed on the track at A. In all tests the dogs tracked only as far as B (as they did in the control test) and then returned to A. All attempts to teach the dog to track along the way where the human was moved above the ground did not succeed.

**Figure 5.5** Konrad Most's float appliance. The tracklayer was pulled forward, just above the ground.

Konrad Most thus concluded that human odor substances falling from above do not produce enough of a track for the dog to follow.

In response to this test, Dr. F.J.J. Buytendijk made the following observation:

> If the human track includes not only footprints but also odor substances that fall down from the human to the ground, then it is possible that this total odor complex is what leads the dog, not only the odors falling down. Most's test does not totally exclude the possibility that, on the normal human track, odors falling from above contribute to the whole smell impression. However, the test indicates that, under these circumstances and within the confines of the test, such odors do not produce by themselves a track that a dog can work out. Even when the people riding on Most's float waved their arms and legs, the dogs did no better at working out the track that only contained odor from above.[6]

Time could be a factor in these tests, because the dogs were put on the track almost immediately. Dust particles and flakes of skin float in the air and need a certain amount of time to reach the ground. Wind can also cause them to fall up to a few yards beside the track. But even in our own experiments, on (much) older tracks, we have not succeeded in getting dogs to work out the part of the track that continued under a float appliance, not even when the person on the float appliance was pulled along very slowly and only a few inches above the ground.

## DROPS OF SAP

In his next experiment, Most hung containers full of liquids on the cable-lift. These containers were designed to drip liquids along the track. Most continued the human foot track with a track made of the odor of a completely different substance (such as drops of juice or tree sap), while the tracklayer was taken in another direction with the float appliance. Even then the police tracking dogs would only follow these new tracks if the containers dropped meat juices or blood. It is clear that such a track must have a biological meaning for dogs (odor of meat, game, or a female dog in heat) for them to follow it readily.

## TRACKS WITHOUT HUMAN ODOR

Finally, Most did tests with his tracking wheel, on which he had affixed wooden and porcelain shoes. When the human track was continued using this wheel (the tracklayer, again on the float appliance, was transported in another direction), even the best police dog followed the wheel-laid track. For Most, it was clear that the damage to the ground surface and the odors of the plants determined the odor of the track. The human odor, according to Most, only added part of the total odor complex. A dog can usually find her way back to her handler based on knowledge of the handler's habits or by following the freshest track, but not always. If there is only one track in a given terrain, the dog may follow this in the

**Figure 5.6**
Konrad Most's
drip containers.

beginning without perceiving the specific human odor. In such a case, the dog can very easily go over to the track of another person, especially if—as in Most's test—it is artificially laid in line with the first track. The question is: how far will the dog overshoot? In Most's test, the "artificial track" was 128 paces, so rather short. In Romanes's tests, however, we know the setter first overshot the branching of the tracks before tracking back.

We also can consider ourselves. When we're absent-minded or distracted, we sometimes walk or drive down the wrong street without noticing. It may take some time before we discover our mistake. How often have you gone all the way home without thinking about it? To suppose that a dog naturally focuses her attention

**Figure 5.7** Konrad Most made artificial tracks with a tracking wheel equipped with wooden shoes, and later on with porcelain shoes.

on the track all the time is illogical. Of course, it is possible to teach a dog to focus attention for a certain time on the track. That requires a strong bond with the dog to pass on this stimulus. It is also important to vary the tracking during training, often changing terrain and conditions.

## THE PURSUIT OF CLEAN-SCENT TRACKING

Most's tests indicated that dogs will follow the track laid by the porcelain shoes as if it were a human track, and that the float, which did not touch the ground, provided no track for the dog to follow. This confirmed Most's earlier opinion that tracking dogs follow the mix of odors from damage to the ground surface, odors of plants, and odors of shoes.

But in 1931, by laying tracks with bare feet on ice, Dr. Hansmann proved that the skin secretions of the feet produce a very good track for the dog to follow.[7]

The question of whether or not dogs could be trained to recognize and follow the odor of the tracklayer out of the total odor complex of the track kept Most busy. Around 1930, after much training, he did indeed succeed in teaching some dogs to stay on the tracks of their handlers, even when those tracks were approached closely and even crossed over by cross-tracks. But it was much more difficult for him to make a dog track-sure on the track of a stranger.

To clarify, Most did not at first employ a start point (a place at the beginning of the track where the track's odor is strong). After he made such starts, his results were immediately better. Although, as Most correctly said, a strongly scented "start" almost never shows up in the practice of police work. Because of the stronger odor at the start, the dog gave more attention to the track she had to follow. As well, the other cross-tracks, younger or older, were suddenly much less interesting to the dog.

In 1938, R. Belleville gave the final assessment—and his recommendation included something that had not been done before.[8] At the beginning of the track, Belleville said, there should be a "start," an olfactory oasis about half a square yard in size, created by standing there for some amount of time and leaving extra odor. If the dog could pick up enough odor there, it could be proved with 86 to 97 percent certainty (under normal ground and weather conditions) that the dog could follow the individual human odor on the track. As well, if this "start" was in place, the dog had a 100 percent probability rate of not going over onto a cross-track, as long as the difference in time between the creation of both tracks was at least 10 minutes. Even if there was a time difference of 3 minutes between creation of the cross-track and laying the correct track, it was still reasonably certain that the dog would stay on the correct track.

## Influence of Fatty Acids

The influence of the fatty acids present in human sweat on tracking was tested by Dr. T. Uchida from Japan in 1953.[9] He used the best Japanese tracking dogs to work out tracks laid according to Most's Tracking Cross. Uchida assessed the work of this group of well-trained German shepherds in order to select the best dogs for the next part of his experiment. The dogs he chose were clean-scent tracking: they were not tempted to follow the wrong track at the cross, and they correctly followed the original track.

For the next tests, Uchida ensured that the tracks were polluted. Tracklayer A wore shoes to which were added butyric acid until the turn, and then he put on his own acid-free shoes. Tracklayer B's shoes were normal until the turn, and then butyric acid was added to them. All tested dogs correctly followed track A, even at the turn; they were not tempted to go over to track B.

During a similar test, a mixture of fatty acids and other substances present in human sweat was put on the shoes instead of butyric acid. In this experiment, the dogs followed the polluted track and went over at the crossing from track A to track B. Some dogs refused to work out the track at all.

Uchida's experiments proved that a good tracking dog cannot only recognize the qualitative and quantitative details in human sweat odor but can also use these details as a guide for tracking. Such a dog will not be tempted from the track by the alteration of one single sweat-odor component. Only when multiple odor components are changed (or used as a distraction) will the good tracker lose confidence in working out the odor details of the track, which is to be expected.

## Y-Scheme Tracks

The dog's ability to determine the differences in odor between the main track and the cross-track was again tested in 1967, during the doctoral research of Paris's Dr. J. Honhon.[10] He did not employ Most's Tracking Cross, however, but instead used a Y-scheme track. At the branch of the Y, the dogs had to decide which track they should follow, the original track or the cross-track.

Honhon determined that the dog's ability to make the right choice depended on the length of the track between the start and the turn, and on the gap in time between the creation of the main track and the cross-track.

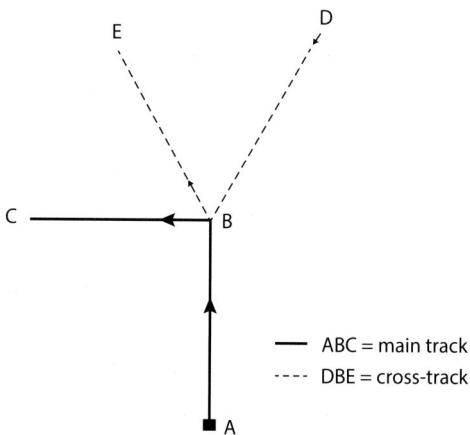

**Figure 5.8** Honhon's Y-scheme. The dog's ability to stay on the track from A to C depended on the length from A to B and the difference in time between when the cross-track D–E was laid and when the main track was laid. The greater the difference in time, the more likely the dog is to follow the track from A to C.

If the first leg was 875 yards (800 m) long, then 75 to 85 percent of the time the dogs stayed on the correct track; if it was only 55 yards (50 m) long, then the dogs chose the correct course in only 45 percent of the cases.

If the difference in time between the creation of the main track and the cross-track was a quarter of an hour, the dogs made the right choice in 65 to 75 percent of the cases. If this difference in time was half an hour, the dogs chose well in 70 to 75 percent of the cases. And if the difference in time was one hour, then in 75 to 85 percent of the cases the main track was followed.

Honhon's research, even with a different track scheme, confirmed the conclusions of the Austrian and German research of the late 1930s.

## Breathing and Scanning Odors

In his 1973 dissertation on the smelling ability of the dog, Dr. Karl Zuschneid used electronic measuring equipment.[11] With these tools, Zuschneid could obtain measurements of respiration in tracking dogs, which were important to his odor physiology research. Zuschneid observed respiration during tracking by paying attention to the movement of the breath in the middle of the dogs' nostrils on which he had placed the ends of two small plastic tubes, which transported a part of the respiration air to the measuring equipment.

First, however, Zuschneid conducted tests without equipment, by which he could determine how long tracks were perceptible to the dogs under certain weather conditions. He also wanted to discover whether or not fatty acids and fatty acid mixes by themselves (in absence of tracklayer odor), formed a smellable track for the dog. He created tracks using different fatty acids and fatty acid mixes, like butyric, proprionic, formic, acetic, and caprionic acids.

In total, five German wirehaired pointers were tested on 60 tracks with lengths between 765 and 1094 yards (700 and

1000 m). Zuschneid's research showed that, among these tracks laid under different conditions, the shortest amount of time a track was perceptible to the dogs was measured on a dry, dusty field, while the track with the longest perceptible time was more than 22 hours and took place in a deciduous wood in autumn with a relative humidity of 70 to 90 percent.

All the dogs tested showed great interest in the fatty acids, although their level of interest clearly depended on the concentration and composition of the fatty acid mix. The dogs could convincingly and without problem follow a 24-hour-old track created by a 1/40 mol dilution (1/40 grammolecule per liter) of butyric acid.

Measurements of the dogs' respiration during tracking was more or less the same in all dogs. The sniffing of the dog was printed on paper as waves that were regularly interrupted by exhalation gusts via the nose. A sniffing frequency and a length of the sniffing period was thus determined. (The sniffing period is the duration of uninterrupted sniffing inspiration between exhalation gusts via the nose.) Four basic patterns could be determined:

1. For simple tracks (for instance, 30-minute-old tracks laid by the handler under favorable conditions), the picture was one of regular sniffing inhalations. The waves of the pressure differences in the nose were often small, which means that the speed of air movement in the nose was low. The exhalation gusts via the nose were powerful and regular. In almost all simple tracks, this respiration picture was consistent from the beginning to the end of the track.

2. The above respiration picture faded away when the track increased in difficulty. The waves of exhalation gusts via the nose became smaller and the time between them increased. In other words, the dog sniffed longer, creating more air pressure in the nose.

3. Tracks at the next level of difficulty resulted in the same picture as the preceding, in principle. The sniffing periods were,

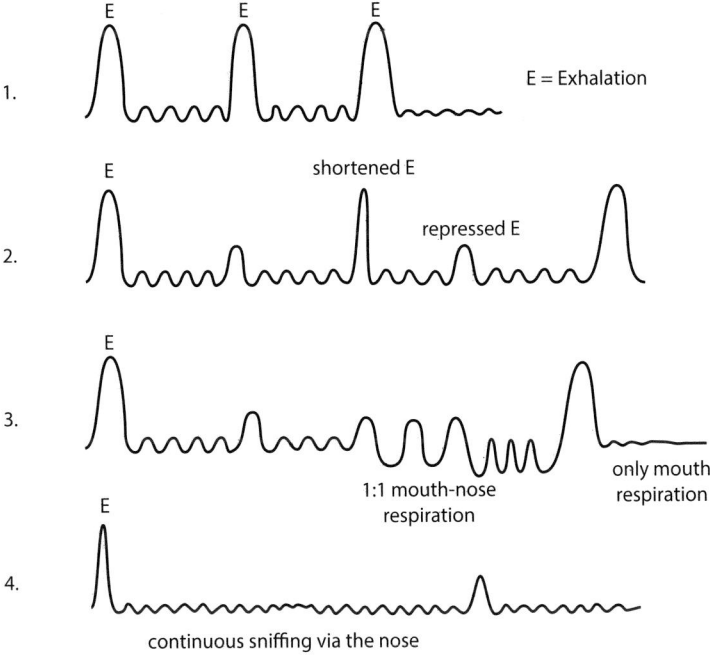

**Figure 5.9** Zuschneid's four phases of sniffing. The basic pattern advances from 1 to 4 as the track becomes more difficult.

however, still longer, and there were short periods during which the dog was obviously breathing through the mouth and nose. It was not unusual to see some dogs exhale via the nose in double gusts.

4. Finally, in the most difficult parts of tracking, the respiration picture showed the dog was almost continuously sniffing. A female dog showed the longest period of continuous sniffing, over 80 seconds long.

Exhaling via the nose probably performs a sort of cleaning of the olfactory cells in the nose's mucous membrane, which is apparently less necessary for odor concentrations that are not high. It looks as though dogs breathe during sniffing in the same way that they do when panting in warm temperatures. But unlike panting, which is mostly ventilation without breathing, high sniffing frequency also contributes to inhalation.

*On simple tracks* dogs easily succeed in combining breathing and scanning for odors. They inhale while sniffing and exhale gustily through the nose.

*When the odor of the track decreases*, the speed of the air current in the nose increases, by which the total of inhaled odor grows. The dog also extends the total duration of the sniffing period. Delayed exhalation then takes place partly via the nose and partly via the slightly open mouth of the tracking dog. The inclination to delay exhaling is a disadvantage for breathing, but longer periods of sniffing allow the dog to gain more information about incoming odors.

*When the difficulty of the track increases* due to extreme conditions, dogs completely suppress exhalation via the nose. While working out tracks that have little odor, dogs often exhale through their mouths, allowing for greater air volumes to pass through the dog's nose and olfactory sensors. Mouth exhalation also takes less time. So, tracking with an open mouth is an advantage, insofar as it allows the dog to spend more time sniffing and scanning odors.

## Sniffing

In 1981, Dr. Walter Neuhaus wrote about the importance of sniffing to the dog's olfaction.[12] The act of sniffing consists of a series of eight to 20 short puffs of inhalation followed by one exhalation. Neuhaus said that during a single puff of inhalation, no whirls of air form in the nasal cavity, as was thought in the past. The space between the nasal turbinates is too small. The small amount and low speed of air sucked in stays under the critical value for current turbulence. The inhaled air does, however, reach the rear parts of the olfactory mucous membrane in the sinuses as a result of differences in pressure in the dog's nose.

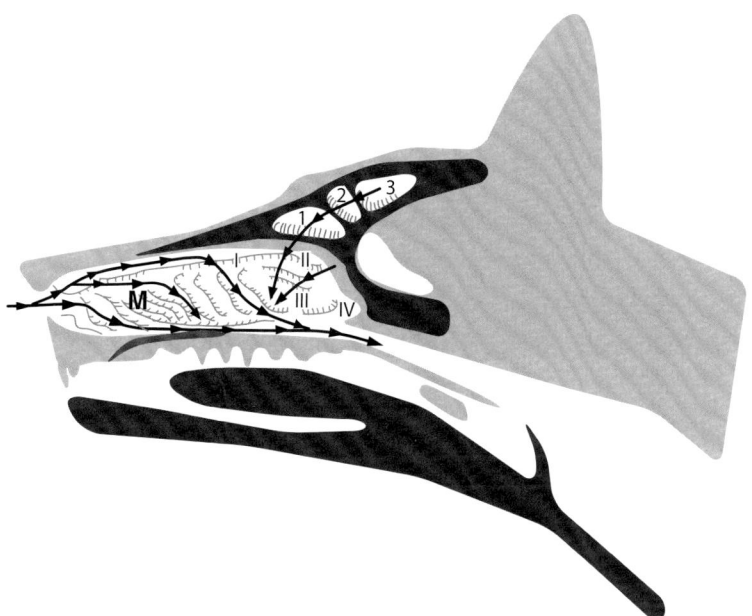

**Figure 5.10** The air current in the dog's nose. The arrows originating from outside the nose indicate inhaled air. Negative pressure arises behind the conchae maxillaris (M). The air flow from the sinuses (1, 2 and 3) and the conchae ethmoidalis (I-IV), indicated by the arrows pointing down and to the left, eliminates the differences in pressure.

Due to the considerable negative pressure behind the conchae maxillaris during inhalation, the dog draws air from the spaces between the conchae ethmoidalis and from the frontal sinuses. At the end of inhalation, scented air flows back into these spaces, so that even the olfactory epithelium—located in the frontal sinuses and remote from the breathing flow—are stimulated.

Diffusion also plays an important part in sniffing. During normal respiration, the pressure difference between inhalation and exhalation in the rear space of the dog's nose is too low to transport odor molecules to the remotest part of the olfactory mucosa. However, molecules diffuse effectively into the frontal sinus if the odor concentration is high enough and if the dog maintains a minimal inhalation time of two seconds.

## The Direction of the Track

In 1993, Aud Thesen and his team at the University of Oslo, Norway, published their research on the dog's ability to determine track direction.[13] The ability to detect the direction of a track is of vital importance to predators, and many modern breeds of dog still have this skill. In Thesen's study, four trained German shepherd tracking dogs were equipped with head microphones that transmitted the sound of their sniffing activity. In all tests, the dogs were handled by their trainers. The tests took place between noon and 3:00 p.m., from May to October 1990, on an airfield near Oslo. The tests were carried out on a dry ground surface on calm days with fair temperatures (59–68°F, 15–20°C). One week before the testing started, a grid of 10-by-4 squares, each square measuring 2.2 yards$^2$ (2 m$^2$), was painted on the ground. All the dogs were video-monitored after being brought at right angles to a track where the position of each footprint was known. The trial began with a dog standing at heel about 5.5 yards (5 m) from, and perpendicular to, the middle of the track. When given the order to track, the dog went straight forward, as she had been trained to do, while sniffing close to the ground. When the dog found the track, she would turn either to the right or to the left.

Three phases could be recognized in the dog's tracking behavior:

1. An initial searching phase, during which the dog tried to find the track;
2. A deciding phase, during which she tried to determine the direction of the track; and
3. A tracking phase, in which she followed the track.

During 10 tests on 20-minute-old tracks on grass, and 10 tests on 3-minute-old tracks on concrete, the dogs always followed the track in the correct direction, meaning in the direction the track was leading. However, the dogs did not always turn the right way when they first found the track. If they at first turned the wrong

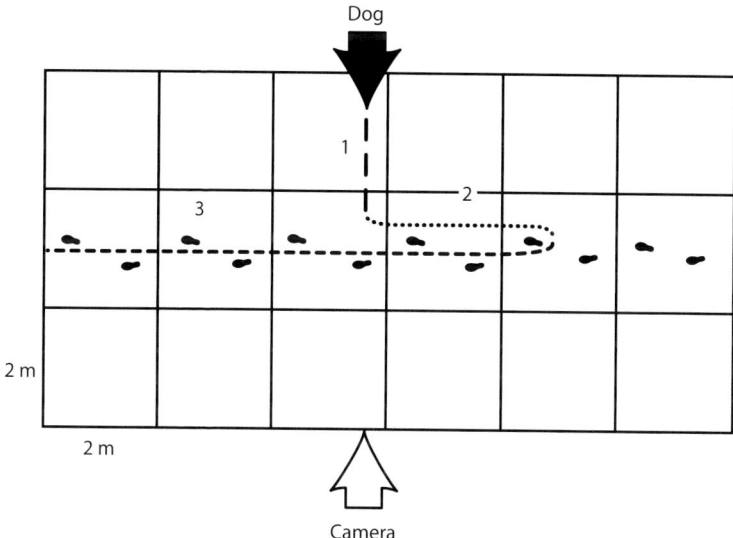

**Figure 5.11** The dog's ability to determine track direction was tested in 2.2-yard² (2-m²) grids. Only 18 of the 40 squares are shown here. This is an example of one dog's route during the searching phase (1), the deciding phase (2), and the tracking phase (3).

way, the dogs turned abruptly and walked in the opposite direction. In the deciding phase, the dogs moved at half-speed, and their periods of sniffing lasted three times as long as during the other two phases. Once the direction was found, they moved faster, suggesting that following the track (the third phase) is a simpler task than determining its direction. The deciding phase seems to be the most difficult one; it is certainly the most impressive one from a human point of view. Over the course of three to five seconds, the dogs needed to smell between two and five footprints and then decide in which direction the track had been laid, regardless of whether or not the track was on grass or concrete (other dogs under different conditions may require more prints).

It would seem that the dogs determined track direction by perceiving differences in the concentration of certain substances deposited by the tracklayer. This implies that, in some of the tests, the dogs must have determined a difference in the concentration of scent in the air above two consecutive footprints that were made one second apart, either three or 20 minutes earlier. To a human, this feat may appear unbelievable. The dog's ability to determine track direction in this time span must mean she has accurate methods of sampling air and a remarkable sensitivity to human odor substances. Dr. W. Neuhaus had already suggested this in 1953, when he said that a dog's detection threshold for acetic acid, an important constituent of human skin secretions, may be a hundred million times lower than the general human threshold.

# 6

# Errors in Mantrailing

In the countryside around Houston, Texas, a five-year-old girl went missing. After eight days, her body was found in a wooded area about six miles (10 km) from her home. She had been violated and strangled. In the vicinity the police found some footprints and car-tire tracks. A dog handler with his bloodhound was asked for assistance.

The way in which the rope was tied around the child's neck immediately made officials suspect a 54-year-old man who a year before was connected to the rape and strangling of a woman but was released due to lack of evidence.

At the crime scene, the bloodhound was allowed to pick up the odor of the rope, the footprints, and the tire tracks, and the dog tracked over a forest path, moving toward Houston. After some miles, the handler decided that his exhausted dog should leave the track and catch a ride along the path in a police car. At each crossing, the dog jumped out of the car, sniffed around, and indicated the direction the officers should drive. In that manner the company arrived at the suspect's house—he, of course, denied any involvement in the matter.

In court, the suspect's lawyer examined the dog handler, who declared that his dog was trained as a "mantrailer" that could work

**Figure 6.1** At the crime scene, the bloodhound was allowed to pick up the scent of the footprints.

**Figure 6.2** The dog tracked over a forest path, moving toward the city.

**Figure 6.3**
The dog handler declared that his dog was trained as a mantrailer and that a bloodhound could work out an eight-day-old track standing on his head.

out an eight-day-old track standing on his head. "Mantrailers can work out tracks of one and a half years or even older, and even follow the scent of someone transported in a car," the handler said.

This handler's claims revived the faith that early 20th-century police and other officials had in search dogs being able to perform remarkable, unbelievable, and impossible tracking feats. Are the claims this handler had about his dog, specifically about his dog's mantrailing skills, realistic, and are dogs indeed able to produce such tremendous performances? It is time to take a closer look at some remarkable cases.

## The Jeffrey Allen Grant Case

During the late night hours of September 18, 1998, a woman from Belmont Shore, near Long Beach, California, was raped by a man she described as white with an "ethnic" accent. She was the seventh victim of rape in that town in 18 months. From a scent pad created at the crime scene, a bloodhound named Tinkerbelle, handled by Dennis Slavin, an urban planner, attempted to track the assailant. Tinkerbelle led the police away from the crime scene to a 20-unit apartment building about two miles (3 km) away. The dog entered the building, went directly to the second floor, and on into the laundry room on that floor. After 10 minutes of attempting to pinpoint the scent, the dog became confused and gave up. She failed to identify any particular unit or individual. Her handler inferred that the building's poor ventilation rendered an accurate alert impossible. The dog did not show any interest in an apartment at any point in the evening.

At the time, Jeffrey Allen Grant, a softball coach, lived in a unit on the first floor, but he was not at home. At no point in the search did Tinkerbelle show any interest in Grant's unit or in the first floor in general. The officers sought to gather more information by questioning residents awakened by the commotion. Grant's apartment first attracted the officers' attention because the light was on in the apartment but no one answered the door when police knocked. Two officers picked the locks on Grant's apartment door with the intention of drawing the occupant outside. When the door did not open, the police testified that they grew even more suspicious and left. In their minds, Grant had become a possible suspect. Later, Tinkerbelle picked out Grant in a scent lineup at the Long Beach Police Department. Jeffrey Allen Grant was arrested as the Belmont Shore rapist and imprisoned. Only three months later did DNA tests prove his innocence; he had nothing to do with this case. The real Belmont Shore rapist, who was caught in 2002, lived in a totally different place.

*Our Conclusion* This was a clear case of an incompetent civilian dog handler using an poorly trained and uncertified dog, whose "proofs" were influenced by erroneous conclusions drawn by the police. Because the handler knew who the suspect was before the lineup, the results of that lineup should have been inadmissible.

## The Anthrax Letters

Just after 9/11, the United States was dealt another blow on September 18, 2001, this time delivered by the fatal bacterium *Bacillus anthracis*. Five people were killed and at least 17 others rendered seriously ill when anonymous letters laced with anthrax spores wreaked havoc in Florida, New York, New Jersey, Washington, DC, and Connecticut. Mail delivery was paralyzed, and the anthrax-laced letters terrified the nation. Because the Federal Bureau of Investigation could find no trace of a perpetrator after six months of investigation, special agent Rex Stockham, an FBI explosives expert who says he has no experience using bloodhounds himself, enlisted the help of three dog handlers and their bloodhounds from Southern California.

Stockham said he first became acquainted with the three handlers after seeing a 1999 video of their experiments taking scents from fragments of exploded bombs. These handlers were Bill Kift, a police officer from Long Beach, California, and his dog Lucy; Dennis Slavin, urban planner and reserve officer with the South Pasadena Police Department, and Tinkerbelle (mentioned above); and Ted Hamm, a civilian who runs his own bloodhound business (assisting in criminal investigations and training bloodhounds and handlers) and is used by the Los Angeles County Sheriff's Department, and his hound Knight.

These handlers took scent samples from objects using a machine called the Scent Transfer Unit (STU-100), originally invented by Bill Tolhurst and further refined and marketed by Larry Harris. The STU resembles a small vacuum cleaner and is designed to draw scent off an article and deposit it onto a sterile gauze pad. This controversial device is criticized because an older scent might linger in the machine when it is pulled out to use on a new case, so the new scent could easily be contaminated and lead to false positives that could botch criminal cases. Gilbert Levy—a defense attorney who also makes an appearance in the Joshua Wade case included later in this chapter—wrote in court filings that the STU-100 has been proven unreliable. It "is not accepted by many in the dog handling law enforcement community," including the Law Enforcement Bloodhound Association and the National Police Bloodhound Association, according to court papers.[1] At least two California homicide convictions based on dog-gathered evidence involving the STU-100 were later overturned.

In this case, the handlers used the STU-100 to take scent from two anthrax-tainted letters half a year after those letters went through the postal system, rubbing against other letters with other scents. In addition, after finding the letters were ridden with anthrax, officials decontaminated them using radiation, which also might have affected their scent. As well, the letters went through lots of hands during the investigation.

Around the time the handlers were preparing to get on the case, scientists in the close-knit, bio-warfare community began suggesting that Dr. Steven J. Hatfill, a disgruntled former employee at Fort Detrick, the nation's premier biodefense lab, was the most likely perpetrator. The press pounced on Hatfill, and the FBI soon became interested in him. According to Mark Miller and Daniel Klaidman in August 2002:

> Early last week FBI agents on the trail of last year's anthrax attacker turned to a 16th-century technology to help solve a 21th-century crime. Agents presented the canines with "scent packs" lifted from anthrax-tainted letters (long since decontaminated) mailed to Sens. Tom Daschle and Patrick Leahy, hoping some faint, telltale trace of the perpetrator's smell still remained months after the fact.[2]

First the bloodhounds Lucy, Knight, and Tinkerbelle visited the homes of people who were possible suspects, in order to see if there was a scent match. They did not respond to most places. But, as Miller and Klaidman reported:

> when the handlers approached the Frederick, MD, apartment building of Dr. Steven J. Hatfill…the dogs immediately became agitated.…"They went crazy," says one law-enforcement source. The agents also brought the bloodhounds to the Washington, DC, apartment of Hatfill's girlfriend and to a Denny's restaurant in Louisiana, where Hatfill had eaten the day before. In both places the dogs jumped and barked, indicating they'd picked up the scent.[3]

As a result, Dr. Hatfill was arrested and a search warrant was issued for his apartment. The investigation netted no direct evidence against Hatfill. He denied having anything to do with the anthrax attacks and said he was pinpointed by investigators because they were desperate to show progress in the case.

On July 27, 2008, Bruce Edwards Ivins, one of Hatfill's former colleagues who worked for 18 years at Fort Detrick, committed suicide before the FBI could file formal charges against him in connection to the anthrax attack. By August 6, 2008, the FBI and the United States Department of Justice formally announced, "The Government had concluded that Ivins was likely to have been solely responsible for the deaths of five persons, and the injury of dozens of others, resulting from the mailings of several anonymous letters to members of Congress and members of the media in September and October, 2001, which letters contained *Bacillus anthracis*, commonly referred to as anthrax."[4]

*Our Conclusion* Again, the investigators in this case allowed the use of uncertified dogs, one of which had already failed in a major case. Furthermore, using the letters—contaminated by other human odors—as a scent source, as well as the suspect STU-100, was problematic. Then, because of the press, handlers also had foreknowledge of Hatfill as a suspect, which led to false alerts from the dogs. All combined to destroy Dr. Hatfill's reputation. Even the $4.6 million settlement Hatfill received to resolve a lawsuit will not erase the status of being a suspect from his mind, or anyone else's.

## The Scott Peterson Case

On December 24, 2002, Laci Peterson, then eight months pregnant, was reported missing from her home in Modesto, California. Soon her husband, Scott Peterson, was suspected of being involved in her disappearance. Four days after she went missing, dogs and civilian dog handlers from the California Rescue Dog Association (CARDA) began a search. The handlers gave Laci's scent to the dogs via a pair of sunglasses taken from the Petersons' house. The handlers did not ask if those sunglasses had been touched by anyone else, such as Scott Peterson, for example.

And so dog handler Cindee Valentin gave her bloodhound Merlin the scent from the sunglasses, after which the dog tracked from the Petersons' home many miles through the city to the intersection at Highway 132, which leads to San Francisco Bay, where Scott had said he was fishing on the day of Laci's disappearance. Valentin said Merlin's search indicated that Laci was taken away from her home in a vehicle, explaining that Merlin did not sniff any sidewalks that day but only followed the scent on a track down the middle of the street. Valentin told detectives that "a trained tracking dog following a scent down the middle of the street is a sure indication a person was in a vehicle."[5]

Near the bay, Eloise Anderson, a member of the Contra Costa Search and Rescue Team and handler of a trailing Labrador retriever named Trimble went on searching. Trimble was brought to the area where Scott said he launched his boat to go fishing, and there Anderson gave Trimble the scent from the sunglasses. As Anderson explained in court, "The dog grew excited. She pulled hard on the leash, taking me out to a pier where she stopped and stared out at

**Figure 6.4** It has never been proven that dogs can follow the track of a person in a moving vehicle.

the water, face into the wind, turned around and gave me the 'end of trail' indication. I stood for a minute to see if she would move on or stick to the end of trail indication. Trimble then gave a 'hard end of trail indication' indicating that Laci was out there somewhere."[6]

*Our Conclusion* Once more, this was a case of using incompetent and uncertified dogs and civilian dog handlers. Using a pair of sunglasses that could also have be handled by the victim's husband or others as the scent article was a big mistake. Valentin's foreknowledge about Scott Peterson's fishing location was also problematic, as was the dog handler's declaration (under oath) that her dog followed that track all by himself for many miles in the middle of a paved road. It is impossible for a dog to follow the track of a person driving in a car; certainly an ability to do this has never been proven in a scientific test. Finally, it isn't even worth discussing Anderson's suggestion that Trimble gave her the "end of trail" indication and pointed his nose to where the missing woman was.

**Figure 6.5** Dog handler Eloise Anderson: "She stared out at the water, face into the wind, turned around and gave me the 'end of trail' indication."

That should immediately have signaled to forensics that this was, indeed, the "end of the line."

## Outrageous Claims

Of course, not only civilians are prone to overstate what their dogs can do. In September 2002, the bloodhounds Lucy, Tinkerbelle, and Knight, along with their handlers, were called to Baton Rouge, Louisiana, to help the FBI find a serial killer.

In an article for New Orleans's *The Times-Picayune*, Steve Ritea discusses a press meeting with Rex Stockham from the FBI Crime Lab in Washington:

> The dogs have been known to pick up a scent up to three years old. "That scent can come from something as small as a shell casing fired from a gun," Stockham said.
>
> Dennis Slavin, the dog handler of Tinkerbelle, said the dogs are also capable of picking out a person's scent from an object even after it has been handled by dozens—perhaps hundreds— of other people. To demonstrate, Ted Hamm, the dog handler of Knight, asked four reporters to touch a sheet of paper and then used a small vacuum (the STU-100) to transfer their scents to a sterile gauze pad. Three of the reporters were asked

**Figure 6.6** Rex Stockham, FBI Crime Lab: The dogs have been known to pick up a scent up to three years old. "That scent can come from something as small as a shell casing fired from a gun."

to stand side by side as a fourth ran around a corner about 250 feet away while the dog sniffed all four scents on the pad. After smelling the three reporters in plain sight, the dog then took off around the corner, let out a howl and ran to the fourth reporter, who was sitting quietly on a low wall.[7]

As if to worsen this "bad joke," Slavin said, "The dogs have performed the same demonstration to find one of 48 people."[8]

## Sandra Anderson, Dog Handler

The work of Sandra Anderson of Midland, Michigan, presents the best American example of law enforcement agencies (local, state, and federal) using a dog handler to assist in criminal investigations without proper and sufficient checking of the handler's qualifications.[9]

Anderson's mixed Doberman named Eagle was believed by law enforcement agencies around the world to be the best cadaver search dog there ever was.

Daniel A. Smith reports that the FBI employed Anderson to search for body parts related to high-profile cases. However, the FBI was warned several times that Anderson was a fraud and that her dog could not do what she claimed he could:

> In April 2002, a law enforcement officer saw Anderson remove a bone from her boot during a search in Oscoda, Michigan, and throw it on the ground. Anderson than claimed Eagle found another bone. This led to an extensive investigation of Anderson and concluded with a ten count indictment in August 2003. Anderson was charged with evidence tampering, obstruction of justice, and lying to investigators. The charges said she not only planted bones in the search areas, but also that she used her own body fluids to stain a hack saw blade, money, and pieces of cloth.[10]

A great number of cases Anderson was involved in underwent appeals.

**Figure 6.7** All dog handlers in forensic investigations should require accreditation and perform according to an identified protocol.

## Penny Bell, Dog Handler

Penny Bell of Milwaukee, Wisconsin, is also a dog handler whose actions are doubtful. She claims her bloodhound Hoover von Vacuum can track a human scent that is more than two months old—even up to two years old—and has claimed responsibility for several successful searches. Bell said Hoover found a body in the Menomonee River in Milwaukee during a 1998 case. According John A. Zautke, a battalion chief with the Milwaukee Fire Department, Bell did not find the body and was not even in the neighborhood when the body was recovered. "Not even close," he said. "She said the dog pinpointed it. This dog stopped every 10 feet along there and drank some water. We have some real good search teams here, and they didn't want anything to do with her."[11]

After his experience with Bell, Zautke instructed police to keep her away from search scenes, where she would show up uninvited and contaminate search sites. Detective Dave Hoeschen of the Stearns County Sheriff's Office agrees with Zautke. Hoeschen said he watched her working with Hoover and has no confidence in her methods. He said she occasionally pulled the dog in the direction she wanted him to go rather than letting Hoover lead. Hoover has no accreditation. But, then, most states, including Minnesota, do not require the accreditation earned after successfully completing specific examinations.

Search-dog expert Terry Shoenbach, quoted by Daniel A. Smith, said he was familiar with Bell and Hoover. He stated there is a lot of controversy surrounding her claims and that there is no way she can do what she claims. "This case is very similar to all the other frauds running around from scene to scene making outrageous claims of finds. This case is very similar to John Preston, Sandra Anderson and the dogs and handlers involved in the Scott Peterson case. These people are not certified by any legitimate canine associations, their claims are unsubstantiated—all they want to see is their name in the paper and in my opinion are out and out liars."[12]

## Keith Pikett, Dog Handler

In the late evening of March 15, 2006, the strangled body of Sally Blackwell, a 53-year-old Texas Child Protective Services worker, was found in a field off Hanselman Road near the city of Victoria, Texas, about five miles (8 km) from her home. After determining the body had been transported there, the Victoria Police Department brought in a team of bloodhounds from the Texas Department of Criminal Justice to search for evidence and attempt to follow the trail. The dogs quickly lost the trail where the field met the road.

Deputy Keith Pikett, from the Fort Bend County Sheriff's Office, and his team of bloodhounds, which had been used statewide to track crime suspects from homicide scenes, were then brought in to pick up the scent. One of his bloodhounds, Quincy, started tracking a scent taken from the body to the Cimarron neighborhood where Sally Blackwell lived. About two miles (3 km) into the trail, Pikett switched dogs. "It's a kind of check if the first dog made a mistake. You see if the second dog picks it up," he said. That bloodhound, James Bond, was given the scent and then led officers first to Sally Blackwell's house and then to former Victoria County Sheriff's Captain Michael Buchanek's house nearby. Some members of the police department already suspected Buchanek, who had briefly dated Blackwell.

Two separate scent lineups were conducted. The dogs were given the homicide-scene scent again, and through verbal and hand cues, were asked to select its match with scents taken from six white males. The dogs selected Buchanek's scent both times. "The dogs are rarely wrong," Pikett said.[13] Four months later, however, it was clear that the DNA found under Sally's fingernails belonged to a 25-year-old Victoria man, Jeffrey Grimsinger, who pleaded

**Figure 6.8** The strangled body was found in a field about five miles (8 km) from her home.

guilty to kidnapping and killing the woman. Grimsinger is serving life in prison.

*Our Conclusion* The police already suspected Captain Michael Buchanek because of a broken relationship with the victim, and their theory was that he transported Sally's body in the trunk of his car to the field. The dogs "tracked" the scent of the victim in the car 24 hours after the track was created, from the field more than five miles over the road, back to her house, and after that to Buchanek's house. We know no dog that can copy this exceptional performance. As well, it is likely that the handler influenced the dogs with verbal and hand cues during the scent lineup.

## Keith Pikett, Dog Handler, II

That Pikett's dogs were "rarely wrong" was, of course, a lie, because for the second time in less than a year, in May 2009, he was sued in federal court for fraud involving his dogs. A special report, "Dog Scent Lineups: A Junk Science Injustice," about Pikett's "highly suspect dog work" was published by the Innocence Project of Texas in September 2009. As Rick Casey, writer for the *Houston Chronicle*, put it in 2009:

> Calvin Lee Miller, a self-employed mechanic and laborer, was called into the Yoakum Police Department for questioning. He took his attorney, Bill Caraway, with him.
>
> According to a lawsuit on Miller's behalf, a police officer grabbed Miller's arm, wiped it "forcibly" with a gauze pad, and said, "That's all I need. Y'all can go now."
>
> The police version is less aggressive, but it is undisputed that the purpose of the encounter was to obtain skin cells that contained Miller's scent so that one of Fort Bend County Deputy Keith Pikett's bloodhounds could check his scent against scents found on evidence connected with two crimes....[14]

The police told attorney Caraway that some local drug dealers had seen Miller buying cocaine. Furthermore, an older local woman told the police she had been robbed by a tall, soft-spoken black man. This imprecise description applies to Miller but also a lot of other men. According to Casey:

> Miller was jailed March 4, based partly on a "scent lineup" conducted by Pikett in which he had his bloodhound compare Miller's scent to scents found on the rape victim's bedcover and items recovered from the robbery.
>
> A DNA test excluded Miller as the rapist in early April, but he wasn't released for more than a month, four days after both victims failed to identify him in a lineup.[15]

*Our Conclusion* When we look at the Innocence Project's view of Pikett, we see some pretty interesting statistics. "Pikett testified under oath that his dog Clue only once erred in 1,659 scent identifications, and James Bond had been wrong once out of 2,266 lineups."[16] Pikett also said that another of his hounds, Quincy, investigated 2,831 scent lineups but only has made three errors. According to the research done by the Dutch police this is absolutely impossible.[17] If it sounds too good to be true, it probably is.

## What Is Mantrailing?

There are three main methods by which search dogs find and track human odors: *tracking* (the dog keeps his nose close to the ground), *air scenting* (the dog holds his nose high to try to find wind-blown human odor), and *mantrailing* (the dog first smells an article replete with human odor and then searches for a matching odor in an area in order to try to find the trail of the person whose odor matches that on the article). When mantrailing, the dog may follow the trail close to the footprints, or more aside or above, depending on weather conditions, terrain circumstances, and the dog's individual preferences.

In principle, any breed of dog can mantrail, but most handlers who do this work prefer to work with bloodhounds. It is said that this breed can follow a track in any terrain, also in towns, and after days or even after weeks. Because the dog follows a certain individual human odor, it said that he has no problem tracking, even in areas that are contaminated by other odors.

### MANTRAILING CERTIFICATIONS

The American Bloodhound Club issues several certifications. In order for a dog to be classified a Mantrailer (MT), he must take a test during which he must work out a trail between 880 and 1320 yards (805 and 1207 m) long. MT trails are at least four hours old and no more than six hours old and include one change of direction, a turn or curve no less than 90°.

The next level of certification is the Mantrailer Intermediate-level (MTI). To pass this test, dogs must work out a trail between 880 and 1320 yards (805 and 1207 m) long. Trails run through moderately scent-contaminated areas (schoolyards, parking lots, etc.). MTI trails are at least eight hours old and no more than 18 hours old and follow a "natural wandering path," including two changes of direction, one of which is a turn of at least 90°. There is one track-layer and at least one cross-tracklayer at the end of the trail, and the team must identify the correct tracklayer.

**Figure 6.9** Just because the dog is a bloodhound does not automatically mean he can track or trail. Even bloodhounds have to be trained carefully.

Finally, the Mantrailer Excellent-level (MTX) test involves a trail that is between approximately 880 and 1320 yards (805 and 1207 m) long that runs through a heavily contaminated area (malls, schoolyards, public parks, forests, industrial areas or similar heavily used areas) that has unlimited access and heavy traffic during all phases of the test (laying and running of trails). MTX trails are between 24 and 36 hours old and, again, follow a natural wandering course, including two changes of direction, one of which must be a turn of at least 90°. MTX trails also have no more than three obstacles (in practice, there are always at least two), such as roads, a water crossing, a bridge, cross-tracks, a contaminated area with another person in it, or a terrain change. There is one tracklayer and at least one cross-tracklayer at the end of the trail, and the team must identify the correct runner.

The American Bloodhound Club asserts that its mantrailing testing process ascertains levels of certification for the sole purpose of sporting events and should not be considered qualification for police or SAR work.

When dogs are being tested, judges pass out the scent articles during trail briefings. The scent articles are either sterile gauze pads or sheets of clean cotton cloth that have been worn by the tracklayer near his or her skin for at least an hour. Handlers are allowed to give their dogs the scent at any time during the test. For the MTI and MTX tests, cross-tracklayers also come into play. All the tracklayers are located at the end of the trail where the dog must identify the right person. The dogs are allowed to air scent, ground scent, or use other means to move along the track as quickly as possible.

Even the highest certified bloodhound, however, has his limits. When asked whether or not a certified bloodhound could work out a seven-week-old scent, Jerry Nichols, the president of the Law Enforcement Bloodhound Association in Denver, Colorado, said, "I don't know any dog, any credible dog…that can do that…

The best chance is within the first 48 hours. After that chances diminish greatly because of time, and because of the elements."[18] Nichols's comments agree with the scientific tests that have been conducted on nose work with dogs on human scent.

## What Can't Mantrailers Do?

For a start, mantrailers—of any breed—definitely cannot perform the unbelievable achievements some have claimed but have never scientifically proven (per the previous chapters in this book).

- Mantrailers cannot follow tracks or trails better than all other well-trained search dogs.
- Mantrailers are not always able to find the track or trail belonging to the scent article at the beginning.
- Mantrailers cannot follow tracks or trails several days old on paved roads in towns.
- Mantrailers cannot follow the tracks or trails of a person transported in a car.

**Figure 6.10** Mantrailers cannot follow tracks or trails better than other well-trained search dogs.

## Testing Mantrailing Dogs

Because we were very interested in the results a police-dog train-ing service claimed its mantrailing dogs could achieve, we were in-vited to visit and to observe some tests. First, we spent an evening with the dog trainers and a biologist from the German University of Munich to discuss what the dogs could do, how they trained the dogs, and why certain practices were followed. We wanted to have a good picture of their training methodology, practices, and work foundation, not to mention an understanding of the research behind their work. The next day, we saw the dogs and handlers at work and observed the methods of tracklaying and working out the tracks.

That night we thought about all we had observed, and the next day we decided that only one of us should conduct the tests. We wanted to create a track for a bloodhound, and we asked if it were possible for the biologist to lay this track. Ruud would walk along the track, but the dog would only get the scent of the biologist. This way, Ruud could decide how the track would be laid, and later on could see the dog and handler at work on the track. The handlers were fine with the suggested manner of working. Ruud refused a city map when they laid the track because he is good at remembering a route. What follows is Ruud's report of the tests.

### THE FIRST TEST

First, I made sure we were alone and that no one was following us, and then I told the biologist not to give any information to anyone about the track. I took him with me and we walked a trail on the right side of the center of the town. I noted the wind direction, and at intersections crucial for the dog's work, we laid the track in such a way that I felt I could predict where a well-trained dog would go. After a nice trail of about 1.5 miles (2.5 km) on paved road (on the outskirts of the town's center), I asked the biologist to stop at a police station. I was sure the dog handlers would react to this well-known location. We phoned the group's coach to come and pick us up there; once again, I asked the biologist not to reveal our route or the end of the track. The handler wanted to work out a track that was at least four hours old, so after being picked up, we worked with other dogs until the handler was ready have his dog work out the track.

When four hours had elapsed, we met at the start of the track. The handler and his bloodhound got ready, and the coach drove the tracklayer (the biologist) to the end of the track at the police station, after which the coach came back to us. I asked how the dog could distinguish between the two tracklayers. Well, that was simple. While the bloodhound took the scent of the biologist (his handkerchief stored in a plastic bag), I stood beside the dog. By this action, without the handler having to issue a command, the dog knew he did not have to follow my scent because I belonged to the group of spectators.

After getting the scent, the dog ran a circle around his handler, set off in the right direction (of course, you could only leave the parking lot via one route), and started tracking. He veered left to right across the road, and after 44 yards (40 m), he came to the first intersection. Immediately the dog chose incorrectly and swung out in the wrong direction. I said nothing but watched the situation and took note of where all the other watching handlers and the coach walked. After about 110 yards (100 m), I asked how the handler knew the dog was following a track at all. We were told that the tail carriage of the dog showed the handler whether or not the dog was on track. At the subsequent crossings, I was always told when the dog had the track, and the handler moved along with him. At one point we were more than two miles (3 km) from the original track on the opposite side of town. If the dog was following a trail, it certainly was not ours. Approximately in the center of town, near the police station, the handler suddenly pulled on the long leash and ran toward the station. There, on the sidewalk, right in sight, the biologist was standing. Everyone was very excited.

"Well, what do you think of us now?" I was asked. I replied that at no time had we following the track, that our track was in fact located upwind, on the other side of the town center. When I was asked how it was possible that we arrived right to the tracklayer in front of the police station, I did not respond. Then I was called a liar, because the handler was convinced that the track the dog was following was ours, and I had given false information.

I could imagine their disappointment, but I waved away all their excuses: that skin rafts were blown off the original track, that these rafts were taken to the other side of the town center (well over half a mile). It was an intense conversation.

## THE SECOND TEST

The next track was simpler. I asked them if it would be difficult for the dogs to find me if I just walked away from the parking area, about half a mile (1 km), then phoned them to start searching after 10 minutes. Well, everyone said that would be a breeze. So we drove to another parking lot in a new city, because my odor molecules and rafts would remain in that town for weeks, they said. Once there, I quickly looked around me and planned the route. Then I walked away. At the end of the parking lot, I whistled and waved sociably, but I did this on purpose to plant the wrong information in their heads about my probable direction. I then laid a track of about 875 yards (800 m), but I followed a completely illogical route. There were no tricks involved, of course—it was actually a long straight track with some simple changes in direction. Along the route in some places, I used red chalk to mark the letter "R."

No one could find me. After 1.5 hours, someone called me and suggested he come pick me up. I suggested, instead, that I walk back to the start. Back at the parking lot, I asked the dog handler to put his dog in the car and show me the trail he had tracked for 1.5 hours with his dog. We did this, and the handler showed me where he was sure the dog was on the track, where they doubted, and where they thought I had been walking. Then we walked back to the cars, and I proceeded to show them my track and the letter marks. I did this throughout the day with all the dogs and their handlers. The handlers were shocked at their performance.

## MORE TESTS

At the end of the day, the group got together to discuss matters. It was clear that they doubted a 10-minute-old track could be too difficult for the dogs, as they always worked on tracks at least 16 hours old. No problem, I said, because I had expected this. I suggested that I go out and lay four tracks in four different towns that we could work out the next day. This way, I thought I could help them completely understand what was wrong with their training methods. We drove to the different towns. It was a hilly landscape, and there were plenty of bridges and viaducts for my purposes. I would start out from parking lots, applying the same tactic (whistling and waving), and then lay the track. I allowed the coach to pick me up at the ends of the tracks, and I was quite sure each of these endpoints would be easy to pass along to the handlers: an old house, a demolition place, a school, and a bus stop.

The next day we went tracking, and every time the coach dropped me off at the endpoints. I would sit quietly on a stone or a bench, but once the coach had driven away, I would run 110 yards (100 m) or so back along my original track and hide behind a car or in the bushes. After a long time I would see the group with the trailing dog arrive. They never came via my original trail—I know this because I could always see them arriving from a completely different direction. The dog and handler always came to the point where I had been dropped off, looked around helplessly, then looked behind cars or in bushes, and then produced their cell phones so they could call me. I answered these calls and always asked them to look in a certain direction, then I came out of hiding. They were very happy, saying they found me, only 110 yards away. But then I pointed to the original track, told them the wind direction, and discussed other points of interest, such as the position of the other handlers and the coach. They did not all walk behind the dog and his handler, but some of them, such as the coach, walked on the other side of the street. It was striking to me that at the intersections, the coach always walked slowly in a certain direction, and the dog and handler also chose that direction.

The sledgehammer blows to their methods had been heavy and precise. After two days of walking out such tracks, all the handlers felt ashamed and were sincerely looking for answers for their dismal results. They themselves could not understand what the problem was.

## TESTING THE SCENT LINEUP

To conclude our visit, we conducted a very simple test that we hoped would explain the Clever Hans Effect. We engaged them in a positive discussion about their training methodology, which is actually very simple: the dog takes odor from a scent marker and has to discriminate odors until he finds the right person. When the dog finds that person, he must report to his handler that he has found a match. Between taking scent from the marker and finding the person, there is usually a track of a certain length and a certain age to work out. I suggested we just forget the track and simply test whether or not the dogs were able to find matches based on a scent marker.

We put three of their men at a row, each 11 yards (10 m) apart. From all three of them, we took a scent marker (a cloth), and we placed each in its own plastic bag. We took care of this, so only we knew which marker belonged to which person. Then we called in the handler and his dog. So, we said, here we have a dog handler offering his dog a scent marker, but in this case no one of you here in the room knows to whom the marker belongs.

For the first time in their training, these dogs were being presented a scent without what had come to be the usual nonverbal cues. There was, thus, no nonverbal communication between the handler and the person whose scent was given or any other person in the room—the dog had to do it all by himself, with his own nose. We asked the handler to tell us if his dog gave an indication of similarity in odor at one of the three persons. We then would tell the handler if the dog was correct or wrong.

We had now seen the dogs at work over the course of three days, so we could have told them in advance what responses their dogs would give. To the surprise and annoyance of the handlers, none of the dogs could find a match. The biologist and the coach (also in the group of people to be matched) were rooted to the spot, astonished.

At one point, the coach was deep in thought and suddenly understood what we were trying to make clear. The biologist still did not understand what happened and could not fathom why the dogs could not successfully complete this simple test. Finally, the handlers were emotional, because they could see their dogs' stress reactions to this trial, which was doomed to fail.

After our visit, the mantrailing project at this training centre was closed down.

## The Scent Article Method Project

In England in 1998, a three-year project conducted by the Essex police and funded by the Home Office started to test the efficacy of the mantrailing method. Bloodhound Sherlock and another bloodhound called Morse—like the BBC television detective—as well as two German shepherds, Scully and Reagan, were enlisted

**Figure 6.11** In a scientific test in 2001, none of the dogs could fulfill the requirements and the SAM project was stopped.

as puppies to be trained in SAM, the Scent Article Method of sniffing out suspects. This was the same method as that used at the training center we visited.

Despite some early successes, the SAM method failed. During the course of a scientific test in 2001, none of the dogs could fulfill the requirements and the project was stopped. Around the same time, bloodhounds and hunting dogs were tested according to the same principles at police-dog schools in Bavaria (Germany) and Vienna (Austria) and all fell short of expectations. Having watched what happened with the SAM test in Essex, the Dutch police decided not to start a training program with bloodhounds and/or mantrailing.

## Bloodhounds and Tracking or Trailing

We do not dispute that bloodhounds can track or trail. Well-trained bloodhounds with the right temperament and training can track or trail as well as any other dog breed. A disadvantage to working with bloodhounds is that they are sometimes stubborn and rather tough if they do not want to work or do not see the point of it. Just because a dog is a bloodhound does not mean he can track or trail. Remember, all dogs have to be trained carefully, a task often under-estimated by beginning dog handlers.

At this point we are reminded of Penny Bell's claim: "basically, bloodhounds don't need any training—it is natural instinct."[19] Bell said she trained Hoover herself after attending a week of seminars and watching television shows, including the *CSI (Crime Scene Investigation)* series. Bell did not attempt to certify Hoover's skills. As she said, "I believe Bloodhounds should not be certified…Why should I be teaching my dog something that it does naturally?"[20]

## Five Big Mistakes in Mantrailing

In mantrailing there are five main causes of faults.

### 1. SKIN RAFTS THEORY

*First* is the unproven theory of Dr. R.J. Clifford, later also published by W.G. Syrotuck, that individual human odor substances (flakes of skin, odor molecules) glide through the air for a long time (and also can stay in one spot for a long time) and can be smelled by dogs for a long time. According to the Clifford/Syrotuck theory, there are about two billion cells on human skin, of which about 1/30 are released daily as flakes of skin, also called rafts. This would mean that, per minute, more than forty thousand cells fall off the human body. Clifford and Syrotuck based their theory on the idea that trailing dogs follow a track of rafts. Further, the theorists suggest that these rafts are moved around by the wind and pile up in certain locations, such as on the windblown side of a building. Supporters of this theory claim that the rafts are blown many miles away from the "track," and can be taken away by cars to other places, but may also for weeks (some say months) stay at certain spots and remain detectable by dogs.

The comprehensive research of police officer Major Konrad Most (as discussed in chapter 4) disputes this theory. As he proved in his experiments, where tracklayers first laid a track on foot, then were pulled away from the track on a floating device, all well-trained tracking dogs stopped tracking at the point where the tracklayers ascended the float and moved away. According to and proven by Most, rafts falling from above do not produce enough of a track for the dog to follow. Based on Most's research and on our own experiments, we believe the Clifford/Syrotuck theory does not hold water.

## 2. CLEVER HANS EFFECT

A *second* important cause of faults in mantrailing is related to the Clever Hans Effect (see chapter 3), named for the horse that waited for his master's unconscious cues in order to tap out correct answers to questions with his hoof. The critic Pfungst deduced that Hans responded to his owner's slight leaning forward as a cue to stop tapping his hoof. People around Hans believed he had correctly answered a question, and Hans got his reward. (See also the experiments of Emilio Rendich, Ádám Miklősi, and Krisztina Soproni, also discussed in chapter 3.)

When handlers overlook the importance of the Clever Hans Effect during training, they may introduce problematic behaviors to their dogs that are difficult to "un-teach." We must know about these cueing experiments in order to fully understand how well our dogs can learn to read us. During training, you want your dog to respond to the relevant cue. So, when searching for human odor, the only cue must be the odor. When we observe trainers and handlers working with their dogs, sometimes their unconscious cues are obvious. For example, an instructor's habit of slightly moving her head when the dog reached the "correct" place on a training field (also the movement of the instructor or other people present) was enough of a cue for dogs to learn and respond to it. But how can we prevent ourselves from cueing the dog in some way, if they can pick up on and respond to such minimal signals? The answer is obvious: work "blind"—do not know the direction or the end of the track, and preferably have no one close by who knows it, since this person may also unconsciously cue the dog.

### 3. CONTAMINATION OF THE SCENT ARTICLE

A *third* fault that easily and often happens in mantrailing is the contamination of the scent article that starts the dog looking for a trail. An article is considered contaminated when it is has odors other than the one the dog needs to sense and know. In the Netherlands, the police follow a strict protocol that dictates how to collect, preserve, and store the scent sample from the crime scene (the *corpus delicti*). That protocol is based on years of methodical observation and scientific research. The protocol begins with the first officers to arrive at a crime scene. These officers are aware of the possibility of dogs being used for scent identification. This awareness prevents the contamination of relevant material. For example, a window may have been opened by a burglar using a crowbar. The crowbar may be very rough, making it impossible to lift fingerprints off it. However, it will certainly contain the odor of the perpetrator who brought the crowbar with him and used it to force the window. The officers at the crime scene must not touch the crowbar. Of course, even if a scent-identification lineup is not in the cards, the crowbar will certainly be taken as a piece of evidence, and attempts will be made to match the marks found on the window frame to the crowbar that was found. When collecting the crowbar for this purpose, there is no harm in touching it. But when collecting the crowbar for scent identification or DNA testing, the (scent and DNA) traces on it need to be left alone so they will not mix with other traces from other humans.

The selection of the item to collect or from which to take a scent sample must be done in an intelligent way. Ideally, officers

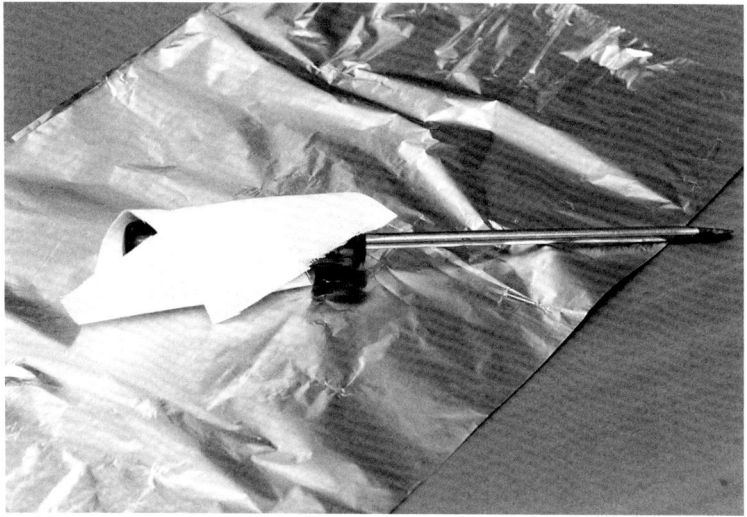

**Figure 6.12** The method for taking a scent sample from an object collected at a crime scene by the Dutch police. (KLPD, 2002)

will select objects that are clearly linked to the crime. Objects that have been brought to the crime scene by the perpetrator are the best, but objects found on the scene of the crime that have certainly been touched by the perpetrator are also good. Wet or dirty objects, objects that several people have touched, or objects that have been lying outside for a couple of days are less desirable, but police do not exclude these, especially if they are significant to the case.

Objects collected at a crime scene are examined in many different ways. The sequence of these tests is worth considering. For example, rubbing an object with absorbent cotton to collect a scent sample will destroy fingerprints. If fingerprints are to be collected, it is better not to rub the object, but instead to drape the cotton loosely over the object. Combining scent-sample collection with DNA analysis can also be problematic. For scent identification, you can collect objects from the crime scene and store them in glass or plastic. However, biological evidence used for DNA-testing should be stored in a paper bag or a cardboard box, because if this material is stored a plastic bag, for instance, the biological trace will eventually mold. You should only use plastic to store items for DNA testing if you freeze the bag, or if the materials can be transferred within 48 hours to the testing lab.

In partnership with forensic laboratories, it is important to integrate proper scent-trace collection into police procedure: Obtaining good scent traces and preserving them properly is imperative to an investigation that involves scent identification. If the objects are relatively small and can be preserved whole, you can place them in thick plastic bags, and then expel as much air as possible out of the bags before tying them with a knot. Objects can also be placed in clean glass jars with twist-off lids. If the object is big and unwieldy, or if it cannot be removed (a car seat, for example), or if the object needs to be used for other purposes, you can take a scent sample. Place a piece of absorbent cotton over the object, then place a piece of aluminum foil over the cotton, and then press the foil down to maximize contact between the object and the cotton. Leave the cotton and foil in place for at least 30 minutes and then remove them, carefully placing the absorbent cotton into a glass jar with a twist-off lid. Scent traces are best stored in rooms with little or no daylight and a relatively constant room temperature. Sunlight is especially detrimental to odor, so it must be avoided. A room with limited access and a proper registration of incoming and outgoing articles is also recommended.

The final prerequisite to proper collection of scent traces is organization. Officers collecting odor traces for scent identification should have the correct material available: the right kind of plastic bags, tweezers, glass jars, scent absorbers, aluminum foil, and sealing materials. Organization and forethought prevents objects from being collected in paper bags or other inappropriate containers.

**Figure 6.13** The correct storage of materials necessary for scent training in the Netherlands. (KLPD, 2002)

## 4. QUALITY OF THE SCENT ARTICLE

A *fourth* important cause of faults in mantrailing is the quality of the odor on the *corpus delicti* or scent article. Consider the following analogy. A fingerprint expert first analyzes the quality of the fingerprints on an object. He or she will know right away if the quality of the fingerprint is insufficient for analysis and comparison with other prints. Fingerprint experts will not work with poor-quality fingerprints; they will only try to make matches based on quality materials. Unfortunately, there is no similar method to measure the quality of the odor left on an object. We know from experiments that dogs can detect human odor on objects even if they have been left outside for days, sometimes weeks. However, this does not mean that the quality of the odor, or the fullness of the scent picture, is sufficient for the dog to be able to identify the person matching the odor. In this way, odor resembles memory, which is vital to cases involving eyewitnesses. There is no way to measure the quality of the witness's memory of the incident. Even so, those who witness crimes are confronted with lineups of people and are asked to identify anyone they recognize from the incident. And as we know, memories can be incorrect.

We also have to be aware that scent traces can only be used once. When they are taken out of their packaging and a dog breathes on them, their odor starts to change. You can repackage the material, of course, but you have to accept that the odor on the object or sample has changed significantly.

### 5. DOG HANDLER EGOS

Finally, the *fifth* problem leading to faults in mantrailing: some dog handlers want to "score" with their dogs no matter what, and even if the task is impossible, they want to prove their dogs can do something special. This, as we know, results in handlers leading their dogs.

## The Joshua Wade Case

On August 3, 2007, Mindy Schloss, a 52-year-old psychiatric nurse from Anchorage, Alaska, vanished. Six days later, her car was found in a parking lot near the airport. On the steering wheel, police found the DNA of her neighbor, Joshua Wade, 27, who in 2003 was acquitted of murdering a woman named Della Brown. In 2000, Wade had also been arrested on felony charges of robbery and burglary, which were later reduced. Wade also had a history of perpetrating small crimes and domestic violence.

At first, police arrested Wade for bank fraud, using Schloss's ATM card on August 5 and 6. He stole $1000 before an ATM machine kept the card. But six weeks later, on September 13, when her partially decomposed body was found in the woods, Wade was charged with the murder. Schloss had been shot and burned.

Two weeks after Mindy Schloss went missing, investigators called in Dennis Slavin and Tinkerbelle, and Bill Kift and Lucy, the handlers and dogs that had failed so dramatically in the Jeffrey Grant Case from 1998, and who were also involved in the 2001 misdirected investigation of Dr. Steven Hatfill. The controversial STU-100 machine was used again. As noted previously, this vacuum-like device sucks in a scent from an object and then deposits it on a cotton pad; dogs use the scented pads to find matching trails.

In several instances in this case, scent samples were collected from items that had not been sufficiently protected (such as the seat of Schloss's car, after numerous people had already been in the car during the investigation), and law enforcement officers failed to exclude all known persons who could have contributed to the scent sample at the beginning of some of the searches.

By the time the dogs were on the case, the tracks were over 12 days old, in an urban environment, and some were several miles long. The bloodhounds followed the scents taken from Schloss's abandoned car and from two ATMs in the center of the city (so a place where a lot of people walk around and interact), where investigators say Wade used her card after her disappearance, straight to Wade's house. One trail stretched over four miles (6 km) and ended directly at the side door of Wade's house. The dogs also followed Wade's scent from the corner of Cutty Sark Street, where Wade and Schloss both lived, to Schloss's car, which was abandoned near the airport.

The dog handlers testified they had used their dogs to rule out involvement by other people in Wade's house. They did this by taking samples of those scents to the site where Schloss's body was recovered in a wooded area in Wasilla. They claimed that "FBI bloodhounds have been trained not to move when given a scent pad if the scent isn't present at a scene."[21] More than two months after Schloss disappeared, the only scent pad that got a response at the crime scene where the body was found came from Wade.

**Figure 6.14** The bloodhounds followed 12-day-old tracks, some of which were over four miles (6 km) long, through an urban environment from two ATMs in the center of the city.

Rex Stockham, supervisor of the FBI's human scent evidence team, worked with the dogs that tracked Wade. In court, Stockham explained:

> The dogs are trained to pick up human scent trails made of odor and sluffed skin cells. They can find trails made by people in cars because the car ventilation system blows out odors. They can also pick up trails of people traveling by bike. Human scent dogs are different from tracking dogs used to find criminals on the run. Those track from footprint to footprint. They're also different from dogs used to find bombs, blood or cadavers.[22]

He continued,

> [Human scent] dogs are trained to find a specific smell. A body scent trail is more diffuse than footprints. It's like dust that settles on surfaces along a trail. The wind can disturb it, pushing it against walls and into cracks, while humidity makes it stick. The trails can last weeks or even months, though they diminish over time. Dogs can also detect specific scents on surfaces that have been submerged in water...[23]

**Figure 6.15** Do you think a dog, even a trained bloodhound, can really pick up a scent and track a man over four miles across town, over a week after he made the trip?

Dennis Slavin, Tinkerbelle's handler, concurred: "Human scent trails are viable for days, weeks and sometimes months. Human scent will be caught up against the edges of buildings, curb lines… and will adhere to things in its path."[24]

*Our Conclusion* After reading this book, do you think a dog, even a trained bloodhound, can really pick up a scent and track a human over four miles across town, over a week after that person made the trip (some of it on a bicycle)? And can a dog correctly trail a suspect in an automobile? For us, this case is significant not because Joshua Wade was innocent (we now know he was guilty) but because of the fraudulent dog search work investigators used to gain a search warrant for Wade's house. As Wade's defense attorney Gilbert Levy said, the handlers and the methods the handlers used led to "notorious false positives." Because of that, Levy said, the dog evidence should not have been heard by a jury, and the search warrant was also perhaps invalid.[25]

# 7

# Human Odor and Dog's Scent Perception

Many factors influence a human scent track. There is damage to soil, often caused by kicking or shuffling; even simply walking on the ground surface causes physical changes and brings out specific scents of plants. Then, there is the scent of footwear, the scent of the materials used to make shoes or boots, shoe polish, and items ground into the soles. Finally, there is the individual human odor from foot sweat, skin rafts, and body odor, which is also very important to other search work, such as scent-identification lineups.

## Scents of the Track

When a person walks across a meadow or field, his or her footprints cause changes that contribute to the scent of the track. Some changes are visible—bent or broken-off parts of grasses, weeds, and twigs, for example. Some are invisible, as when footsteps disturb, damage, or kill insects and microorganisms. Further, the pressure of the human body on the ground, and the friction resulting from walking warms the ground, causing the scent to rise.

### SOIL

The tracklayer's footwear applies pressure to the ground, pressing into it more or less depending on the tracklayer's weight and the

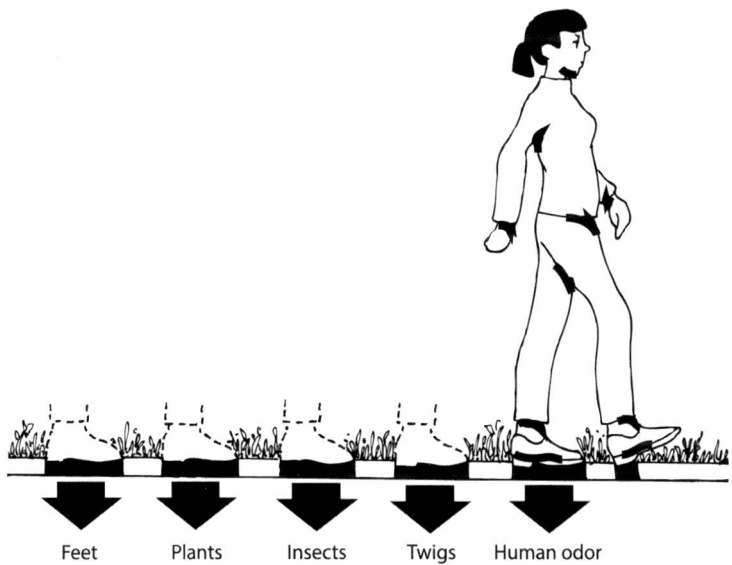

**Figure 7.1** When you create a track, the weight of your body presses down on the soil, and plants, twigs, and insects are damaged, releasing odors particular to each. These smells, combined with those of bacteria and the smell of your feet —which comes through your shoes or boots and stays for a while on the ground—create an olfactory sensation for dogs.

composition of the soil. On plowed land, the tracklayer's footprint can normally be clearly seen because it causes visible damage to the ground surface. Because of this damage to the ground, humidity and biological odors are released from the earth. Bacteria from organic matter breaking down in the soil also gives it a certain scent. The pressure of footsteps and warmth from resulting friction causes this scent to rise—think of the smell you experience when digging in your garden.

## PLANTS

With every step the tracklayer also causes changes to live plants. Just as every soil has its own characteristic scent, plants, weeds, grasses, and flowers have their own specific scents. Damaging parts of plants sets free a scent of various saps, which also influence the scent of the track. Anyone who has taken leaves off a geranium knows what we mean by setting free a scent after damaging a plant. A recently mown lawn also has a specific scent we recognize. We humans have a high threshold for most smells, but for dogs the damage caused by one footstep on plant growth is more than enough to smell sap. The scents that exist after plants and grasses are damaged are, just like that of soil damage, almost immediately detectable because they are borne in the air. The intensity of these scents is highest when the track is fresh.

The flow of sap stops after a certain period because microorganisms in and on plants help them recover from damage. "Wounds" inflicted on plants close quickly, just like a scratch on your skin, and dead or dying-off parts are cleared away by bacteria that make things rot. The result of bacteria's work on plants and in soil is a stench like that of a dung heap or the odor of a haystack. Anyone who has ever smelled a pile of grass left out in the rain for a day knows the rotting smell we are talking about. Dogs are able to clearly sense this smell and follow it.

### BACTERIA AND OTHER ORGANISMS

Damaged or dead insects and other tiny organisms underfoot on the track also impart their own scents. Bacteria does its work best when the environment is warm and humid. When someone walks, the pressure of their feet and the friction of walking warms up the ground, and footfalls damaging the ground releases humidity from the soil, creating optimal conditions for bacteria to set to work. Of course, the relatively small amount of warmth and humidity caused by tracklaying does not last long, so the weather plays a greater role in how long a scent lasts.

Bacteria will work on the damage inflicted by a tracklayer for as long as temperature and humidity levels allow. High and extremely low temperatures decrease bacterial reproduction, delaying their action. Bacteria also thrive more in humid than dry air. Bacteria also play an important role in human odors, so we can partly determine the ideal weather conditions for tracking. Optimal conditions for bacteria include average to high humidity levels in the air, and the temperature should be neither too high nor too low. Temperatures around 68°F (20°C), measured about 1.5 yards above ground, are ideal.

## FOOTWEAR

Any type of footwear can be worn by a tracklayer. Of course, rubber, leather, and any other materials used in footwear have their own specific scents, which together form the specific scent of the footwear. Added to that are the chemical scents of finishes, protective sprays, and shoe polishes. Another thing tracklayers leave behind are small bits of the soles, especially on a hard surface; these bits also contribute to the scent complex of the track, as do the scents of anything stuck to the soles of the tracklayer's shoes. These may be pleasant scents for the dog, or they could be repulsive scents to work with and thus make tracking difficult. During tracking we have to remember that as the terrain (or soil) changes, some of the last sort of ground walked on will stick to the tracklayer's footwear and will be transferred onto the first few feet of the new part of the track terrain. If the tracklayer walks through a meadow and onto a road, for example, some odors of plants—possibly even bits of plants—will carry over onto the beginning of the track on the road.

## HUMAN ODOR ON THE TRACK

Some trainers still believe that the individual odor of the tracklayer plays no particular role in a dog's work. According to them, other factors determine the smellable track: the scent of footwear, and differences in shoe size and the weight of tracklayers, who sink more or less into the soil, damage plants, and in doing so cause

**Figure 7.2** Rubber, leather, and all other materials in footwear each have their specific scents.

**Figure 7.3** In searching for an individual human odor on the track, this Dutch police dog stays on course, even over hard road surfaces.

more or less strong scents. In their opinion, the odor of the track-layer exists in such a small quantity on the track that it will virtually disappear into the other scent components. Other trainers and handlers believe individual human odor is what dogs search for on the track. They think that human odor is what keeps dogs on track, even over hard road surfaces and when tempted by cross-tracks made around the same time as the main track.

So is it or is it not possible for the dog to perceive the human odor component on a track? In 1953, to determine whether or not a dog could successfully do this, Dr. Walter Neuhaus calculated human sweat production and sweat odors. These he compared with the dog's very low threshold values for odors, which he had already determined in earlier experiments.[1] Neuhaus concluded that the amount of human odor on normal tracks, even after hours, was enough to be perceptible to the dog. This conclusion was based on the threshold values for separate, clear odor substances.

But human odor is a mixture of odors. So as a follow up, three years later, Dr. Neuhaus investigated the prickle threshold of receptors stimulated by complexes of odors, and he found lower threshold values for such mixtures than if the different substances were offered separately.[2] His earlier conclusion that dogs could perceive human odor was therefore strengthened. Neuhaus found that even if an odor was surrounded by another strong scent, the dog could observe little deviations in the odor mix. This agrees with the observation that a dog can recognize the odor of a human and an article touched by that human, even when this article itself has a stronger scent, or has another strong scent on it.

Dogs encounter mixed scents when working out a track; they also encounter changes of scent when they shift from a meadow to a wood, for example. Even when the other scent components of the track are about a thousand times stronger than the human odor, it is still possible for the dog to recognize the individual human odor in the track.[3]

## The Human Scent Complex

All mammals produce several different odors. Expired air, urine, feces, exocrine glandular secretions, and body openings all contain odorous substances. We will focus on the odor of the skin since that is usually the odor that forms a track or a trail, or that is left on objects at a crime scene. In general, skin odor is thought to be the sum of genetic differences, bacterial action, diet, and glandular secretions. In the skin, glands secrete odorous compounds directly onto the skin or into canals that lead to the skin surface. The scent of skin compounds left on a glass slide as a result of fingerprinting remain discernable to dogs for some weeks without having to be preserved in a specific way.

The skin itself is also a continuous source of rafts: dead cells that flake off the surface as new skin cells are manufactured. We leave rafts behind on everything we touch. If sufficient material is left behind, DNA technology can be used to analyze mitochondrial DNA sequences in the rafts and thus identify their owner. Rafts also flake off into the air and are carried away with air currents. (As noted in chapter 5, a whole theory of mantrailing is based on these airborne rafts.) The air currents around the human body transport rafts. According to Syrotuck, these currents have a speed of 1.4 miles (2.3 km) per hour and carry rafts up to 16 inches (40 cm) above the head, from whence they descend.

### INDIVIDUAL HUMAN ODOR

There are differences between odors that come from body openings, human skin, perspiration (sweat) glands, and sebaceous (sebum) glands. In addition to these odors are scents on the human body (and clothing) that result from outside influences such as environment, diet, topical applications (soaps, creams, deodorants), and medications.

People who work in places like butcher shops, bakeries, farms, or labs or factories have occupational odors. The use of soap and foot powders, and ingesting certain medicines and foods also influence human odor.

## ODORS FROM BODY OPENINGS

Odors from body openings (mouth, nose, ears, anus, and the urogenital area) influence individual human odors. While these odors may not be part of the scent complex on a human track, they can play a role for search-and-rescue (SAR) dogs, which search for people under rubble and snow. In particular, the breath exhaled and urine sometimes lost during moments of panic or excitement can provide important odor sources for the SAR dog.

## HUMAN SKIN

The skin protects against influences from outside the body. The upper, or outside, layer is called the epidermis and consists of two types of cells: melanocytes, which are the pigment cells, and the keratinocytes. In the basal layers of the skin, called the stratum germinativum, columnar epithelial cells divide and move outward. These cells pass through several cell layers to the skin's surface, called the stratum corneum. During this process, they first grow, then form keratohyalin (a protein structure), and finally die. It is thought that lipids—free fatty acids, cholesterol, and ceramides—in the stratum corneum form the physical skin barrier. In the stratum corneum, the cells gradually flatten, shrink, and lay loosely against each other. They become keratin and peel off at a rate of 0.02 to 0.04 ounces (0.5–1 g) of dead skin cells (rafts) per day. The epidermis varies in thickness but is normally only a thin membrane. (Where the skin is callused, like the palms of the hands and the soles of the feet, the epidermis is much thicker.) As a result of the continuous renewal of the epidermal cells from within and the peeling off on the surface, the epidermis renews about once a month. The rafts that flake off from the surface are normally tiny and invisible, except on the scalp (dandruff) and as a consequence of skin diseases such as psoriasis.

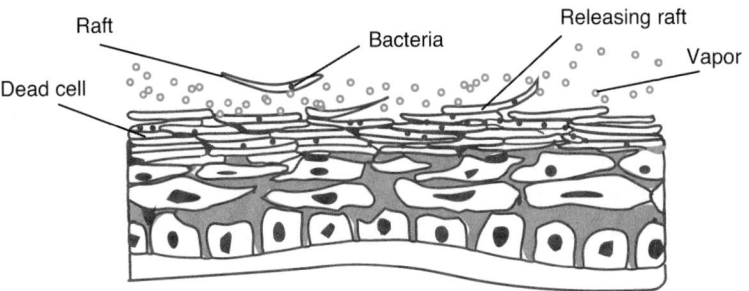

**Figure 7.4** The upper human skin cells gradually flatten, shrink, and lay increasingly loosely against each other. They become keratin, which peels off at a rate of 0.02 to 0.04 ounces (0.5–1 g) rafts per day.

The second skin layer is called the corium (or dermis). The corium is a layer of connective tissue up to one eighth of an inch (3 mm) thick. The top layer of the corium, immediately below the epidermis, is the papillary dermis, and the contact area between the two layers of the corium has a wavy pattern with bulges that connect the layers. The bulges are filled with many little blood vessels (capillaries) that provide food to the epidermis and carry away waste. Further down in the corium is the reticular dermis, which constitutes the bulk of the corium. The reticular dermis contains the muscles around hairs and a network of bigger blood and lymph vessels, which also supply the sebaceous and sweat glands. The reticular dermis is characterized by dense collagenous and elastic connective tissue. The blood vessels in the skin are responsible not only for providing nourishment and oxygen to the skin, but also for regulating body temperature. In the corium there are also a large number of nerve endings, which control the senses of touch, pain, and temperature.

Underneath these layers is the subcutis with adipose tissue, which has important functions in heat insulation and energy storage, and which acts as a physical buffer against shocks and other impacts.

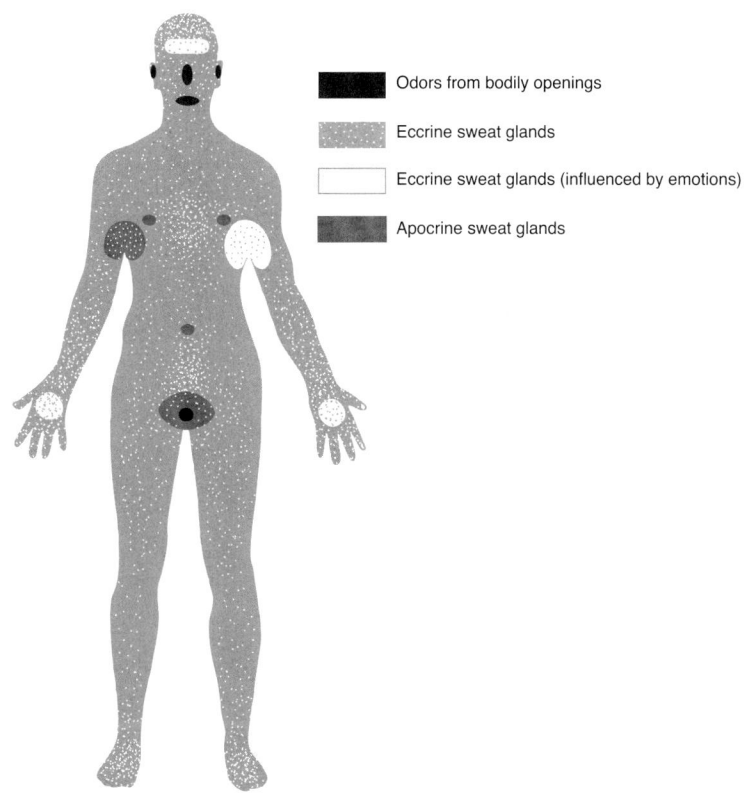

Odors from bodily openings

Eccrine sweat glands

Eccrine sweat glands (influenced by emotions)

Apocrine sweat glands

**Figure 7.5** Distribution of the different sweat glands over the human body.

## SKIN GLANDS

In the skin we find, besides hair follicles, sweat glands and sebum glands that secrete onto the skin, and therefore contribute to odor on the skin. The sweat glands can be divided into two types: eccrine and apocrine.

### ECCRINE SWEAT GLANDS

There are between 2 and 4 million eccrine sweat glands on the body, which produce a clear, watery solution. More than 98 percent of this solution consists of water in which numerous organic and inorganic components are dissolved. Eccrine sweat plays a major role in the thermoregulation of the body. Because of body warmth and the air current around the body, the sweat solution evaporates immediately after it leaves the pores and comes out on the skin. When the body is sweating heavily, clothing that touches the skin will absorb it. During emotional or nervous moments, eccrine glands in the forehead, the palms of the hands, and the soles of the feet secrete extra sweat. In average individuals, the glands can secrete as much as two to four liquid quarts (2–4 L) per hour.

## APOCRINE SWEAT GLANDS

Apocrine glands are found in specific places on the human body, especially in the armpits and genital area. They produce a cloudy, viscous solution containing large amounts of cholesterol. Bacteria on the skin break apocrine sweat down into odorous molecules, in particular steroids, which are thought to be biologically interesting signals. According to Spielman and his colleagues, the armpits, where apocrine glands are abundant, are the source of human primer-type pheromones, the volatile smell substances that get the attention of the other gender.[4] Spielman finds support for this assertion in the similarity between the chemistry of these human odors with non-human mammalian signaling odors. The axillary organ, as this bundling of apocrine glands in the armpit area is called, is not equally present in all human beings: some people have larger axillary organs than others. Those with Asian ancestry, for example, often have small or even absent axillary organs. These glands in the armpits are the major source of body odor as perceived by other people.

## SEBACEOUS GLANDS

Sebaceous glands occur all over the body except on the palms of the hands and the soles of the feet. They are located beside hair follicles and discharge secretions into those structures. The sebum they produce seals hair shafts, thereby preventing the penetration of bacteria and the loss of water. Sebum consists of all sorts of fatty substances that keep the skin pliable and hydrated. When we move our bodies, sebum spreads over the surface of our skin, and so also comes to the palms of our hands and soles of our feet.

On average, there are about 100 sebaceous glands per square half inch (1 cm$^2$). The number of these glands increases to almost one thousand per square half inch on the middle of our chests, on our backs, and on our faces and scalps. People who produce a lot of sebum often have to manage greasy hair.

The sebaceous glands are a type of holocrine gland, which means they secrete whole cells that have broken down to transport them from the body. Sebaceous glands secrete sebum by partially breaking down and releasing a gland cell through a pore in the skin. In the pores, the sebum and the remains of the cell are further broken down by lypolisis, a process driven by enzymes derived from the epidermis and bacteria. It takes eight to 10 days from formation of the cell until it has broken down, and its products (mainly triglycerides and free fatty acids) can be found on the skin. These fatty acid products are thought to form the olfactory signature of an individual. Support for this comes from examining non-human mammals' scent-marking glands; glands known to provide information about the identity of an individual produce sebaceous lipids.

### UNIQUE HUMAN SCENTS

It seems that the lipids on human skin are the substances most likely to cause each person to have a unique scent, so they merit some attention. For the most part, lipids are the products of sebum, produced by sebaceous glands. The small number of lipids on the skin that are not part of sebum come from the epidermis and from contamination (for example, through shaking hands), which can be minimized by frequent washing.

As mentioned above, sebaceous glands are holocrine glands, in fact, the only holocrine glands in the human body. Some of the lipids in sebum are cell lipids (or epidermal lipids) and others are specialized lipids synthesized by the cell (endogeneous lipids). This synthesized part is thought to have the most influence on the composition of the secreted sebum. Approximately 37 percent of the fatty acids found on the skin are "biologically valuable"; the remaining 63 percent consist of more than two hundred different kinds of free fatty acids ranging from very small to very large (C7 to C30[5]). Some of these are unusual; for example, sebaleic acid seems to be a surface lipid that is unique to human skin.

## ODOR PRODUCTION

The products of both the apocrine and sebaceous glands are broken down into odorous compounds by bacteria in skin pores and on the skin. The skin's microflora includes such bacteria as micrococcadeae, staphylococci, corynebacterium acnes, pityrosporum ovale, pityrosporum acnes, pityrosporum granulosum, and propionibacteria. Several studies, such as one conducted by E.A. Eady and associates in 1994, have shown that treatment of the skin with topical antibiotics decreases bacterial populations and thus contributes to a loss of fatty acids.[6] However, some bacteria remain unaffected by antibiotics, probably because they are present in the hair follicles and out of reach.

Different bacterial populations are found in different body areas, and these populations remain quite stable over time.[7] Regional population differences of these bacteria mean different areas of an individual's body have different odors. The regions with the largest numbers of bacteria are the face, the neck, the armpits, and the groin, as well as the soles of the feet and between the toes. Bear in mind, however, that the differences in bacterial population between people are quite large.

## EFFECTS OF AGE

With increasing age, human skin's microflora undergoes qualitative changes, probably because of hormonal changes and changes in sebum production. As children grow up, streptococci populations disappear and coryneform bacteria populations increase. The latter type of bacteria is mainly responsible for odor production. Anaerobic propionibacteria are more numerous in juveniles and young adults than any other age group. Only coryneform bacteria are able to produce axillary odor through the decomposition of apocrine sweat.

The chemical content of skin lipids changes with age. In 2001, R.S. Ramatowski summarized these changes, which include rates of sebum secretion and the amounts of certain fatty acids. Ramatowski also concluded that some components of sebum do not change significantly as the body ages.[8] Young children do not produce much sebum, and their lipid composition is dominated by cholesterol and cholesterol esters, which are primarily of epidermal origin.

As hormonal stimulation increases in puberty, however, more sebum is produced. Peak production happens when a person reaches his or her mid-thirties. Females have lower sebum secretion levels than males, and people with acne have higher secretion levels than people without acne. The stimulation of the sebaceous glands results in a change in lipid composition on the skin: more endogeneously (or internally) produced lipids are found. The epidermal lipids remain relatively constant. Overall, the secretion levels and sebum composition remain constant from puberty until much later in life (males over 70, females over 50). The principle reason for the decline in later life is diminished hormonal stimulation.

## EFFECT OF GENETICS

Researchers who compared the lipid composition of identical twins and unrelated people found evidence for genetic control of lipid composition.[9] This work on lipids and genes relates to other research being conducted relative to genetic control of body odors.

A large body of work about the genetic control of urine odors has shown the significant role of the major histocompatability complex (MHC).[10] The MHC is a group of genes connected to the immune system. In humans it is called Human Leucocyte Antigen (HLA), and the genes are located on chromosome 7. Nowadays, theories about the genetic control of odors include the interactions between immune system antigens and bacteria: the antigens (or their breakdown products) could influence the commensal bacterial flora and thus individual body odor. This area of study could be important for forensic scientists working with odors. As Boyse stated, "Odor profiles governed by HLA could be more distinctive than fingerprints with respect to genetic identity, because the genetic component of fingerprints is uncertain."[11]

Regional differences in microflora on the skin mean that different body parts have their own particular odors. To humans, armpit odor smells totally different from genital odor, which in turn smells different from the soles of the feet. In fact, Löhner found that for humans, the similarity of scent between the same regions of different people seems to be greater than that of different regions of the same person.[12]

This does not mean that an individual does not have a unique odor, however; in fact, Löhner found that for dogs, the similarity in the smell of different body areas of the same person was greater than the similarity of odors between the same areas belonging to different people.

There is also some evidence that the dog's ability to focus on an individual's one, overarching odor is the result of training. Doctors Brisbin and Austad found that dogs trained to detect the hand odor of their handlers had difficulty when asked to choose between the hand odor of a stranger and a non-hand odor (for example, odor from the crook of the elbow) of their handler, and dogs familiar with matching objects scented in pockets to the hand odor of the individual who had handled the objects performed better in trials than in trials where dogs had to match the hand odor of an individual to that of the same person's odor coming from the crook of the elbow.

The importance of genetics to human odor is also evident in the results of behavioral studies in which the difference between the odors of identical twins, siblings, or other genetically related people was shown to be smaller than differences between odors of non-related people. The stability of this "typical" odor is also clear from these studies: for example, siblings recognize each other's odor on T-shirts after not having seen each other for more than two years.[13] It is now generally accepted that there is a genetic base for unique human odor.

## Stability of Odor

For forensic purposes, the stability of an odor over time is vitally important. Although no experiments have been undertaken to try to specifically alter an individual's odor, it seems unlikely that one could alter one's own unique odor: if a person's genetic makeup influences the microflora responsible for the composition of fatty acids on the skin, the only way to change the scent would be to change one's bacterial microflora. Products that minimize axillary odor by modifying the microflora there to produce less odor, are, of course, ongoing sources of income for the pharmaceutical and cosmetics industries, and they illustrate the difficulty of masking or minimizing such odor. Research has found that applying antibiotics to the skin diminishes bacterial populations, but these are usually only applied locally, so the rest of the body continues to generate odors.

Although a person's diet seems to have an effect on his or her odor, lipids derived from diet are in the minority, and the long turnover time of the sebaceous cells (between eight and 10 days) prevents rapid changes as a result of food intake.

Washing also minimizes the amount of lipids on the skin, and therefore odor, but the effect is only short term because lipids are replenished quickly. Human odor is therefore pervasive and stable.

## FACTORS AFFECTING SCENT STABILITY

The odor traces left on objects connected to a crime must be stable to be of any use to forensic experts, since the period between when the perpetrator deposited the odor and when comparisons are made between that odor and that of a suspect can be considerable, from weeks to years. In general, scent marks that linger for a long time are produced by sebaceous glands, but even these odors have a best-before date, and environmental conditions can affect how long an odor remains stable on an object.

Direct sunlight, in particular, breaks down many organic substances, and some microorganisms (bacteria and fungi) feed on organic components like those in odors. In a study done by the Pacific Northwest National Laboratory, researchers examined the chemical changes in latent fingerprint deposits over a 30-day period. They found that saturated fatty compounds remain relatively stable. However, unsaturated lipids (such as squalene and some of the fatty acids) diminished substantially within the 30-day period, especially during the first week. With time, more saturated, low-molecular acids appeared, originating from the breaking down of the unsaturated lipids. In aged samples, the saturated components dominated.[14]

The essential question for forensic purposes is this: how long can human odor on an object retain its unique identity for a dog? The fingerprint study noted above has been confirmed by dog instructors who have observed dogs while teaching them to make scent-identification matches based on aged objects. Dogs have to be trained step by step to make scent identification matches with

**Figure 7.6** On overgrown, moistened soil, well-trained dogs can work out a track up to 36 hours old.

objects aged up to a week, a task that seems relatively difficult for dogs. However, as soon as a dog is trained to deal with week-old scents on objects, she can easily manage scent matches with objects holding much older scents.

## Dogs' Scent Perception

Each human being acquires his or her own (individual) odor. These odors can periodically be of different strengths and composition. Dogs can identify scent matches in human sweat diluted a million-fold.

On moistened sand, well-trained dogs can work out a track of human odor about 12 hours old, and if the track is on overgrown, moistened soil, they can work out the scents for up to 36 hours from the time the track was laid. Even if the track is washed out by heavy rainfall and after intensive radiation from the sun, a dog's scent perception is still successful up to 6 hours after the track was laid.

The sense of smell, like the sense of taste, is one of the chemical senses. In liquid or gas form, scent prickles exert themselves on the nose and its parts. These prickles then are changed into signals the brain can understand, which then allows the animal to respond correctly.

## INSIDE THE DOG'S NOSE

Inside the dog's nose are two kinds of epithelium: the respiratory epithelium and the olfactory epithelium. The respiratory epithelium has small hairs and is coated with mucus. Its function is to clean, moisten, and warm incoming air to body temperature.

### OLFACTORY EPITHELIUM

The olfactory epithelium is located deep inside the nose, next to the cribriform plate, and is darkly pigmented. It covers several bony plates called ethmoid bones and covers a large surface. Different animals have different-sized olfactory epitheliums. There is also a variation in size between the olfactory epitheliums of different breeds of dogs, but there is no direct link between the size of the dog and the size of the olfactory epithelium. However, there is no simple relationship between the size of the olfactory epithelium and sensitivity to odors. An animal with a large olfactory epithelium is not automatically more sensitive to odors than an animal with a smaller one. While a German shepherd has an olfactory epithelium that is 59 to 67 square inches (150–170 cm$^2$), the average human has an olfactory epithelium about two inches square (5 cm$^2$). Yet some odors can be smelled equally well by human and dog, but when faced with other odors, dogs are 10,000 times more sensitive than humans.

An important and unique characteristic of the olfactory epithelium is its continuous regeneration: neurons in the epithelium live 30 to 60 days and then die and are replaced by new neurons. This means that when the olfactory epithelium is damaged, it can completely recover in one to two months. This ability to regenerate is not the same in other sensory organs.

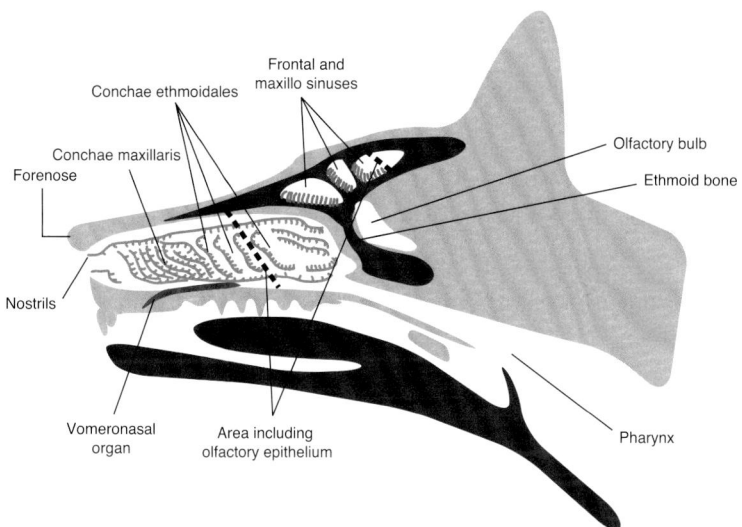

**Figure 7.7** Anatomy of the dog's nose. With every in- and exhalation through the nose, the dog guides odors to the turbinates (also called conchae) and the olfactory epithelium.

Odor molecules can reach the olfactory epithelium by way of the nose or the mouth. The olfactory epithelium is covered with mucus. In this mucus there are small hairs (cilia), and on these hairs are the olfactory receptors. The cilia are extensions of the olfactory sensory neurons in the epithelium. The density of these sensory neurons differs between species and also changes over the course of an animal's lifetime. When a young animal grows up, the density of the sensory neurons (and sensitivity to odors) increases, but as the animal ages, the density (and the sensitivity) decreases. So sensitivity to odors is affected by age. Besides the olfactory sensory neurons, the olfactory epithelium also contains supporting cells and basal cells. The sensory neurons terminate in a nerve that passes through the cribriform plate to the olfactory bulb in the brain. In the brain the nerves are bundled in knots called glomeruli.

*VOMERONASAL ORGAN*

Deep inside their noses, many animals, including dogs, have a second organ that is sensitive to odors: the vomeronasal organ, which is situated in the nose above the roof of the mouth and enters by way of a small canal into the mouth cavity. This organ is very small and difficult to locate, which is why it was ignored for a long time. The sensory cells in the epithelium of the vomeronasal organ have different receptors than those in the olfactory epithelium of the nose. The vomeronasal organ has approximately one hundred different kinds of receptors. Odors do not reach the vomeronasal organ by chance; in fact, it appears that physical contact with the odor source is necessary for transport into the vomeronasal organ. To this end, several animals show what is called the flehmen response (curling their upper lip in such a way that the nose opening closes) after having licked at an odor source. Other, similar smelling behaviors have also been described for animals that do not display the flehmen response.

The probable function of the vomeronasal organ is a sexual one: detecting so-called pheromones, odors that have a strong biological significance for the animal. Pheromones contain information about sex, reproductive state, and dominance. These odors can also lead to physiological changes in the animal. In humans, females who have regular odor contact with males have a shorter menstrual cycle than females who do not. As well, the menstrual cycles of women who live together, such as nuns, or students who live in all-female houses on campus, become synchronized, and it seems this is regulated by odor cues.

## ODOR RECEPTORS

Odor molecules float around in the air, and the odor receptors that can react to these molecules are hidden deep inside the nose. The main route these molecules take toward the receptors is through the nose, but odor molecules can also travel from the mouth up

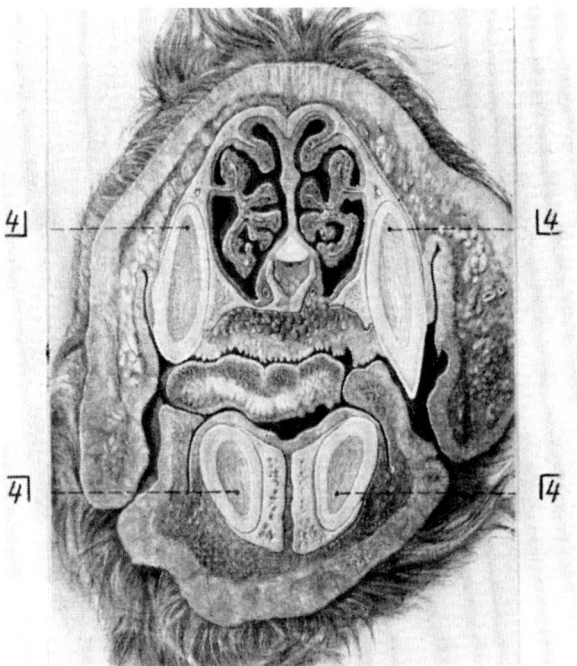

**Figure 7.8** Transverse section of the muzzle near the canines (4) in the upper and lower jaw of a ten-month-old Airedale terrier female. In the upper part are the right and left nasal cavities. The mucous membrane–covered conchae maxillaris is visible. (Courtesy J. Bodingbauer)

through the throat to the nasal cavity and reach the odor receptors in that way. When sitting calmly, a dog breathes in and out approximately 15 times per minute. When walking calmly, the frequency rises to 31 times per minute. During this ordinary breathing, the largest amount of air goes to the lungs via the quickest route, and the odor molecules in this air do not generally reach the odor receptors in the olfactory epithelium. During normal breathing, odor molecules only reach that area if their concentration in the air is very high. Odor molecules reach the olfactory epithelium when dogs (humans, too) actively sniff. When a dog sniffs, the inhalation/exhalation frequency rises to 140–200 times per minute.

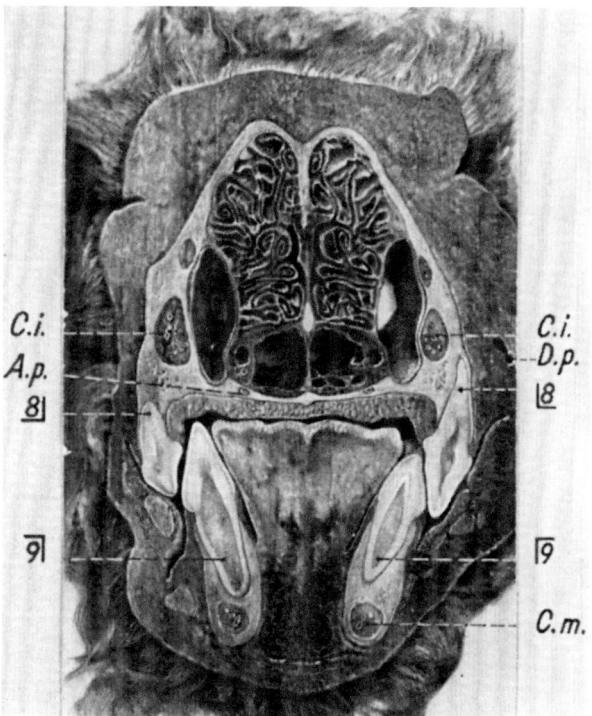

**Figure 7.9** Transverse section of the muzzle of the same Airedale terrier female. Between the first molar in the upper jaw (8) and the fourth premolar in the lower jaw (9) you can see the extension of the olfactory epithelium–covered conchae ethmoidalis. (Courtesy J. Bodingbauer)

The sniffing leads to differences in air pressure in the nose. In the end, air, including odor molecules, enters into the depths of all the nasal cavities.

Tracking and trailing dogs also employ another technique to perceive odors: air scenting, which involves one long inhalation, lasting 20 times longer than ordinary, breathing inhalation. During this long nasal inhalation, dogs exhale through their mouths. This method likely allows for optimal presentation of odor molecules to the receptors in the olfactory epithelium. Measurements of the breathing pattern of dogs during tracking revealed that as a track increased in difficulty, the dogs' sniffing frequency increased. The duration of the sniffing bouts also increased.

The odor receptors that pick up the signals in odor molecules are located on cilia in the mucus that covers the olfactory epithelium. This mucus is watery and contains different agents that cleanse the air; for example, it contains antibodies to different bacteria, as well as detoxifying enzymes. To reach the olfactory receptors, odor molecules must first dissolve in this watery mucus.

But because odor molecules do not dissolve well in water, the mucus contains certain proteins (olfactory binding proteins, or OBPs) that function as carriers, aiding in the dissolution of the odor molecules. The odor molecules thus attach to these proteins, dissolve in the mucus, and are transported to the olfactory receptors located on the cilia of the olfactory sensory neurons. There are probably around one thousand different kinds of olfactory receptors, divided into at least four zones, and all dogs seem to have the same ones.[15] Consider that the eye has three different kinds of receptors (cones) that make it possible for us to see the variety of color that we do. Similarly, the tongue has receptors that allow us to experience five different tastes: sweet, bitter, salty, sour, and umami.

Every olfactory sensory neuron has several cilia with receptors. We think that all the cilia located on a single olfactory sensory neuron have the same type of olfactory receptor.[16] Olfactory sensory neurons that carry the cilia and receptors live for 30 to 60 days, die, and are replaced by new neurons. At some stage during the development of a new neuron, the type of receptor it carries is determined. If a neuron with a type-A receptor, for example, dies, this does not automatically lead to the replacement neuron having the same type of receptor. Rather, the type of receptor that is generated on the new replacement neuron is (partly) triggered by the odors the animal most often smells. Wang, Wysocki, and Gold (1993), and Youngentob and Kent (1995) found that animals systematically trained on certain odors develop more receptors for those odors.[17]

Research thus suggests that each type of receptor reacts to a certain part of an odor molecule: a certain shape or chemical group. To simplify things for our purposes here, we will assume that part of different kinds of odor molecules is the same and as a result stimulates the same kind of receptor. However, each odor molecule also has several different parts that each stimulate different receptor types. So a single odor will stimulate a specific group of receptor types; each odor stimulates a different group. In this way, one thousand different kinds of odor receptors can differentiate clearly amongst a large number of odors.

## FROM NOSE TO BRAIN

As soon as a receptor has reacted to an odor signal, the olfactory sensory neuron fires and an impulse is carried through the nerve to the bulbus olfactorius, the olfactory center in the brain, located directly behind the cribriform plate. The pathway between the brain and the receptor is extremely short: the sensory neuron that has the receptors on cilia at one end is the same neuron (or nerve) that delivers the impulse to the brain. Such short impulse pathways are unique to the olfactory system: in all other sensory organs the signal must be passed along to at least one other nerve—sometimes several nerves make up a pathway—before the signal reaches the brain.

Olfactory nerves converge in one to two thousand nerve-knots called glomeruli, located in the first layer in the bulbus olfactorius. The nerve ends of sensory cells that have the same type of olfactory receptor all come together in the same glomerulus. Sensory cells of a certain receptor type, therefore, have a matching glomerulus in the brain.

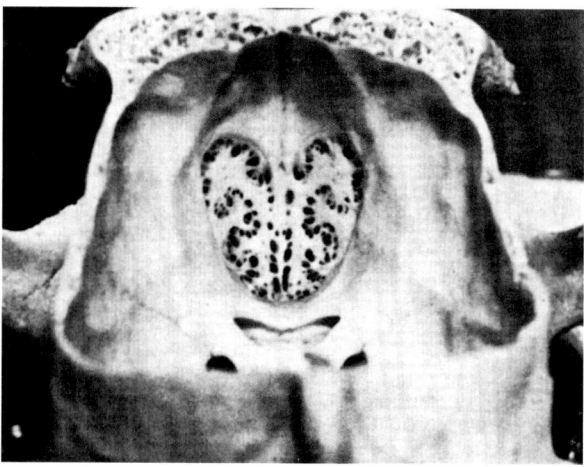

**Figure 7.10** The cribriform plate of the ethmoid bone, as seen from inside a dog's skull. Olfactory nerves enter the brain through openings in this plate. The cribriform plate of the dog is very large, accommodating an enormous number of olfactory nerves. (Courtesy J. Bodingbauer)

Because the information from many olfactory sensory neurons comes together in a single matching glomerulus in the brain, the signal is amplified in the brain. Even if only a few sensory cells are triggered by an odor, the information that odor imparts is bundled in the first layer of glomeruli in the olfactory center, and this layer can then project a clear signal to the second layer of glomeruli deeper in the bulbus olfactorius.

As previously noted, in the olfactory epithelium, sensory cells having the same receptor type are distributed evenly within a zone. Each zone in the epithelium connects with a zone in the bulbus olfactorius. Sensory cells of the same receptor type all connect to the same glomerulus. In this manner, a clear spatial pattern emerges: each odor stimulates a characteristic spatial pattern of glomeruli in the brain.

The development of the glomeruli in the bulbus olfactorius is partly determined by the kinds of odors an animal comes across most often. If you train your dog on one particular odor, for example, he will develop more olfactory sensory neurons for that particular odor, and the matching glomeruli also become more developed.

The information from the first layer of glomeruli in the bulbus olfactorius is passed on to a second layer of glomeruli. The glomeruli in this second layer are interconnected, which leads to better perception of minute differences. This makes the signal clearer. The glomeruli in this second layer are also influenced by experience.

## CEREBRAL CORTEX AND LIMBIC SYSTEM

The signals that reach the bulbus olfactorius follow two paths for further processing in the brain. One path leads to the cerebral cortex, also called "gray matter," the outer covering of the cerebrum and cerebellum. When the information imparted by the odor reaches the cortex, the animal becomes aware of the odor, knows he or she has smelled something, perhaps recognizes the odor, and if so will react or not react to the odor. This series of events, from awareness to reaction, is called cognitive processing of information.

The other path leads deep into the brain to an area called the limbic system. The limbic system is responsible for many autonomic, unconscious processes, such as emotions, sexual behavior, and some physiologic responses. Experiments with humans have shown that even though a person's brain reacts to an odor, he or she may not be conscious of smelling something. The processing of olfactory information by the limbic system is called non-cognitive processing. The limbic system receives odor information through the main olfactory epithelium and from the vomeronasal organ.

Through the limbic system, odors can have a physical impact on animals. The odor of lemons counters depression in rats. The odor of a human male shortens the menstrual cycle of the human female. The odor of a strange male leads to a spontaneous abortion in a rat that has just become pregnant by another male. Some odors stimulate animals; others slow them down.

The limbic system processes information quickly, before processing happens in the cortex. This means that the non-cognitive effects of odors processed in the limbic system may interfere with cognitive processing in the cortex. A good example of this taken from police practice is the reaction of a dog to the odor of a member of the kennel staff. Using the odor of this staff member as a foil in a scent-identification lineup often leads to mistakes. This can be explained by the direct, positive association the dog has with this person's odor: food, being taken for a walk, attention, praise, and so on. The dog may react to this person's odor before she "realizes"

**Figure 7.11** Asking members of kennel staff to create cross-tracks for training dogs often leads to mistakes. This can be explained by the direct positive association the kennel dogs have with the staff member's odor. The dogs may react to this odor before realizing they are actually supposed to be looking for a different one.

she is actually looking for a different odor. The reverse problem can also be explained in this way: an odor a dog finds "difficult" to work with may be one she has negative associations with, resulting in avoidance behavior.

Another example of non-cognitive processing of odors interfering with cognitive processing is the reaction of a male dog to the scent of a female dog in heat. Her odor, as processed by the limbic system, initiates a sexual behavior pattern. Even though a dog can be taught not follow through with the behavior, his first reaction to the odor will always be present because of his drive to procreate.

The olfactory organ is not static; it continuously regenerates, and it reacts to differences in the environment. When an animal is confronted with a certain odor often, physical differences result in the olfactory organ. These changes can be seen on all levels: more sensory cells with certain types of receptors, larger glomeruli, and permanent changes in the brain. As well, when an animal is not in contact with certain odors, her olfactory organ will be less able to perceive them.

# 8

# Scent Problems and Training Problems

In general, all sensory organs work in the same way. Each sense organ has receptors. These receptors are located in or on sensory neurons. The receptors react to a signal in the environment. This signal stimulates the sensory neuron and results in an impulse. This impulse can be seen as an electric current, running from the sensory neuron through the nerves. The impulse is transmitted from one nerve to the other, until it reaches the brain and the information is processed.

Problems in perception can occur at any of the stages, from reception to processing. Perhaps the signal cannot reach the receptor, or there is no receptor available for a certain kind of signal. Maybe the sensory neuron does not react, or the nerve does not react. Finally, even though the scent has been received and passed along to the brain, perhaps the brain interprets the information incorrectly.

Every olfactory sensory neuron has a single kind of olfactory receptor. Olfactory receptors are continuously renewed together with their olfactory sensory neuron. The number of olfactory receptors for a particular scent is adjusted to how often a scent is smelled. An animal has a lot of olfactory receptors for scents smelled regularly. To optimize your dog's nose, you should engage in continuous scent training.

**Figure 8.1** The number of olfactory receptors for a particular scent is adjusted to how often a scent is smelled. This suggests that to optimize the nose of your dog, you need to engage in continuous scent training.

## Odor and Odorless

It is relatively easy to prove that something has an odor. If a person can smell it, or if you can train an animal to react to it, then it has an odor. But it is much more difficult to prove that something has no odor at all. Maybe a person with a very sensitive nose could smell the odor, or maybe the animal you trained to detect the odor was not trained correctly.

And there is another problem when it comes to measuring odors. One study on people used electroencephalograms (EEG) to establish characteristic brain-wave patterns that result when people smell an odor. During the study, researchers found that sometimes a person's brain reacts in the characteristic way to an odor, but the person may say he or she has not smelled anything.[1]

We must be aware that terms like "odor" and "odorless" are difficult to define, and we must use them with care. Many substances that seem odorless to us can be perceived by dogs. "Odorless" may not exist.

In order to strip an object of its odor, it is not enough to boil it in water because odor molecules do not dissolve well in water. When cleaning objects, use (non-perfumed) soap or another fat-dissolving product, and after that rinse well with clean water.

Remember that certain porous substances absorb and retain odor (sometimes for a long time). Many dog handlers have made the mistake of punishing their dogs because they thought the odor on the training object (or in a particular place on the training field) was no longer present, only to discover later that in all probability the odor persisted. While conducting scent training with your dog, keep in mind the possibility of your dog sensing related or remnant odors.

## Temperature and Scent

Temperature plays an important role in the perception of odors. Warm substances give off more odor in cold surroundings than warm substances in hot surroundings. It is more difficult to find

**Figure 8.2** Many dog handlers have made the mistake of punishing their dogs because they thought there was no more odor present, only to discover later that in all probability an odor persisted.

a cold article by its smell when the ambient temperature is low. Substances or articles that already give off recognizable odor under normal circumstances smell stronger when they become warmer. Warm foods, as you know, smell much stronger than cold foods. As well, freezing a warm food, such as a steak, causes its smells to decrease so that it hardly smells at all. The steak will still give off a recognizable smell while frozen; it releases a minute amount of odor into the air, which, when breathed in and warmed up in our noses, penetrates the olfactory epithelium and its odor receptors.

## Alternating Perception

Human nostrils alternate every few hours. A slight swelling closes the nostrils in turns, and the closed one lets less air through than the open one. According to Noam Sobel and his colleagues at University of California, Berkeley, these changes in air current also have consequences for scent discrimination.[2] Sobel asked 20 people to smell a mix of carvon (found in caraway and the rind of mandarin) and octane (which smells like petroleum). Seventeen of the 20 people found the mix smelled more like carvon than octane when they smelled with the "active" nostril, and the opposite when they used the inactive one. After a few hours, as the nostrils alternated, the same happened. The differences in smell were not caused by just the left or right nostril. These alternations may also happen in the dog's nose, which may explain why dogs sometimes hesitate to recognize an odor.

## Factors Affecting Olfactory Perception in Dogs

The dog's physical condition can change her ability to perceive scents. In some cases, the dog will find it difficult or even impossible to smell odors. Common colds or the influenza virus can affect the sense of smell. Humans and dogs with these illnesses have a decreased ability to perceive scents. Dogs that have been infected by the influenza virus, but that do not yet show normal symptoms, already have a decreased olfactory sensitivity. Even the beginning of an infection such as kennel cough can lead to a diminished sense of smell.

Other illnesses that can diminish a dog's olfactory system are renal failure, hypothyroidism, and, more often present in dogs, Cushing's syndrome (an adrenal hypersecretion). Problems with the upper teeth, such as root infections, can also influence the dog's ability to smell. As well, certain medications, especially antibiotics, can affect odor perception.

In general, female dogs have a more acute sense of smell than males, although hormonal circumstances can influence their scent perception. Being in heat or approaching being in heat can affect both her sense of smell and her ability to concentrate. Sensing a female in heat in the neighborhood, or changes in the pack order, can also affect other dogs' sense of smell.

The color of a dog's coat can also indicate his olfaction ability. Albino or pale colored dogs' ability to smell may be diminished in part, or in full. This may explain why albino animals in the wild have a low chance of survival, partly because of their marked white color and partly because they are unable to distinguish odors very well.

Short-nosed breeds often experience problems with searching because of breathing problems. Boxers, for instance, can search as well as other working dogs, but they need more stops to rest.

The smaller breeds are thought to have a disadvantage because they have a smaller olfactory area. In practice, however, it has been shown that small dogs can easily perform as good search dogs.

## Adaptation and Nose-Fatigue

The precise way in which a scent signal triggers a reaction in the olfactory receptor is unknown. Somehow this scent signal leads to the firing of an impulse, which can be compared to an electric current transmitted through the long nerve all the way to the brain. When a certain sensory cell is continuously triggered to fire, it

**Figure 8.3** Short-nosed breeds often experience problems with search work because of respiratory problems. But boxers can track as well as other working dogs; they just need more rest stops on long tracks.

begins to adapt. Adaptation is the adjustment of the sensory cell to weaker or stronger sensory signals. If a sensory cell is continuously stimulated in a certain way, it will cease to react to the stimulus. For example, if you enter a room where people are smoking, you notice the smell of cigarette smoke when you come in, but after a while you do not notice it any more. If you go out, and let your nose rest for a bit, then re-enter the room, you will smell the smoke again. A dog's sensory perception also adapts along these lines.

Dogs and humans do not smell only with their noses. The olfactory epithelium is only one part of the perception of odor, the organ that scans the air for scent. The prickles coming in via the cilia turn into signals brought to the olfactory bulb. The brain then ensures that these signals lead to the right scent impression. We are, in fact, smelling with our brains.

## FAST ADAPTATION

Adaptation in the olfactory system is manifested on two levels. The fast adaptation (achieved in less than one second) is the quick change from active to passive response during continuous stimulation, which is physical and happens at the sensory neuron level. Fast adaptation may be related to the decrease (within a fraction of a second) of scent perception upon cessation of breathing during a sniff, as was documented by R.W. Moncrieff.

When a scent is removed from the air over the epithelium after the sensory organ has been stimulation by it for a long time, the sensory response diminishes from active level to zero within a few hundred milliseconds. Such relatively fast turnoff is essential for a sensory mechanism that responds to changes occurring between consecutive sniffs.

## SLOW ADAPTATION

The second level is slow adaptation (over the course of one minute), which is a kind of mental tiredness, also called "nose-fatigue." This is the slow suppression of perceived odor intensity during prolonged exposure arising from central neuronal processing.

**Figure 8.4** Slow adaptation is a kind of mental tiredness, also called nose-fatigue.

**Figure 8.5** When a dog is tracking with his nose right on the surface of the track, his nose may adapt to the odor. By deviating from the track, he can "clear his nose" and be able to smell the scent on the track again.

## IMPLICATIONS OF ADAPTATION FOR SEARCH DOGS

When working with search dogs, you may come across situations where adaptation plays a role. Following are some examples:

- The density of narcotic odor in a room where a lot of a certain narcotic has been hidden, or where a smaller amount has been hidden for a long time, can be intense. In a room like this, a search dog may have a hard time indicating the exact source of the odor, especially if he has been in the room for some time. The dog's sensory cells have adapted; they have been stimulated so much that they no longer react to the smell. Of course, a decrease in the magnitude of concentration of odor in such an odor-saturated environment can also explain why a dog cannot locate an odor's source. Dogs know how to handle this situation: they will want to go outside to get a breath of fresh air and then come inside again. In some cases, the dog must go away and come back a few times before he can pinpoint the scent clue or source.

- When a SAR dog locates an odor in the rubble, he sometimes may go away from that place and then return, refreshed, better able to pinpoint the scent clue.

- When a dog is tracking with his nose right on the surface of the track, his sensory cells can adapt to the track's odor. By raising his head from the track and then returning to it, he may "clear his nose" and be able to smell the scent on the track again.

If you punish your dog for refreshing his nose, as we have seen happen in sport training, your dog will deliver a less-than-satisfactory result. Or, he will start putting his nose to the ground and act as though he is searching or tracking, without actually doing so.

### CROSS-ADAPTION

Another aspect of adaptation is cross-adaptation. This happens when one has adapted to a certain odor and it becomes impossible to smell certain other odors. This phenomenon has been described in scientific research for several odors, but not all cross-adaptations are known.[3]

We also know that certain chemicals—for instance, acetone and xylol—can block a great swathe of olfactory cells or push aside other scent substances. If you first smell acetone and then xylol, you can clearly perceive both odors. However, if you reverse the order, smelling the xylol first, you will find that you cannot perceive the acetone for some time.

Handlers of detector dogs especially have to be aware of this. They also must think about the fact that other substances, such as ether or petrol, can fill up the dog's nose with odor, so that it can be more or less blocked for several minutes. The dog's ability to determine finer odors becomes very difficult during that period.

Both dogs' and humans' ability to smell is also disturbed by irritants and strong and abnormal odor prickles. Tracking on a meadow strewn with fertilizer or, for detector dogs, in a chemical-scent-laden factory or laboratory, may disturb the sensory cells. To ensure your dog can work even in such circumstances, train him on as many odors as possible and under constantly changing circumstances.

## Scent and Memory

The sense of smell is firmly connected to learning and memory. Homesickness, for example, will occur in children partly because of unfamiliar odors. A child who has access to a familiar smell—a cuddly toy or blanket—when away from home, however, may be able to avoid feeling glum. This same principle works with puppies, too. When you bring a new puppy home, make sure you also bring along a toy or piece of cloth that smells like the litter; the well-known smell of this item will help put your puppy at ease in his new world of strange odors.

Odors not only bring back memories, but they can also stir up memories of events long buried, even thought to be forgotten. There are cases of people who could not remember anything about their nursery school days until they sniffed a typical school odor and were able to recall images of the school, teachers, other children, even specific games played or other events. This connection between odor and memory also may explain why a dog can recognize, even after many years, a previous owner.

Even the lofty astronaut needs the smells of home when out and about on long travels in a relatively odorless environment. Researchers have tried to improve quality of life in space by providing astronauts with little bottles that contain familiar odors associated with good memories.

## Failure Scents

Some scents can become associated with failure, leading to poor performance. During tests, people were given a difficult task, which they could not do well, and at the same time they were exposed to an unusual odor.[4] Subsequently, when asked to complete an easy, ordinary task with the same odor present, they had difficulty succeeding. The participants in this experiment had come to associate the odor with failure.

Dogs, too, can inadvertently make the same connections between difficult searches and "failure" odors, such as the smell of certain types of soil or even the odor of certain tracklayers.

**Figure 8.6** Dogs can connect certain problems in searching or tracking with a "failure scent," such as the smell of certain types of soil or the odor of certain tracklayers.

## Aging and Hormonal Changes

An individual's smelling ability varies over time and is influenced by, among other things, hormonal variation, age, and illness. In general, the females of a species have a more sensitive sense of smell than males, but for both genders, overall sensitivity decreases with age. There are also large individual differences, not only in people, but also in other animals, such as dogs. A single individual may also react more sensitively at one time than at another, which may be the result of fluctuating hormone levels.

## Amount of Scent

Differences in amount of scent appear to be perceived by animals as differences in kind of scent: a lot of one scent simply smells differently than a small amount of the same scent. This phenomenon is also known from tests of hearing: a very loudly played C-tone sounds different from a very soft C-tone. In 1988, Gross-Isseroff and Lancet established that perception of different amounts of scent lead to qualitatively different processes in the brain.[5] A small amount of a scent does not lead to a correspondingly weak reaction compared to a large amount of the same scent, but to a completely different reaction. It follows that when training your dog on a scent, you should use varying amounts to get him used to smelling different amounts. When a dog is used to finding only small amounts of a scent, he may not recognize a large amount of the same substance because it smells different from what he has learned.

## Complex Scents

Training animals to discriminate between scents is more difficult when the scents are complex (combinations of different scents)

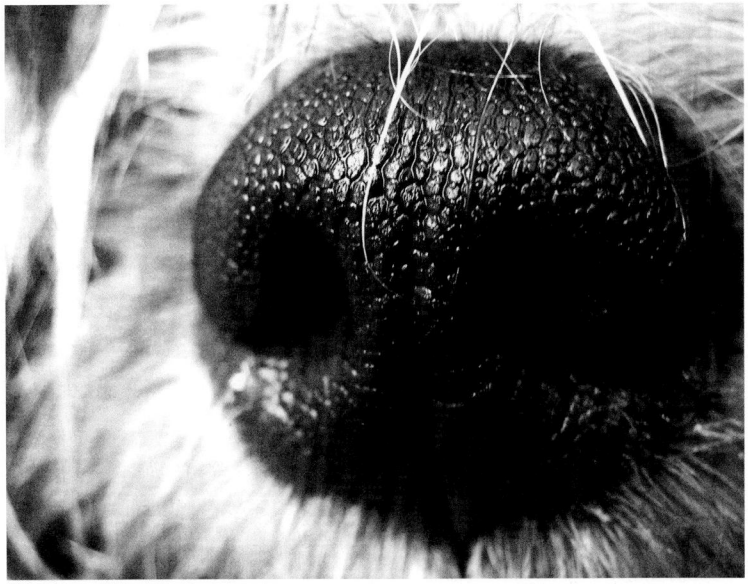

**Figure 8.7** When a dog is used to finding only small amounts of a particular scent, he may not recognize a large amount of the same scent, which simply smells different from what he has learned.

than when the scents are single scents. In 1989, Laing and colleagues demonstrated that if a scent is presented alone, an animal is much more sensitive to it than if the same scent is presented as part of a complex.[6] This is something to be aware of in training: even if your dog is capable of finding a very small amount of a "pure" odor, he may have problems when he has to find this same small amount as part of a complex of odors.

When training your dog to recognize and follow complex odors, remember that complex scents are learned as a unit. Staubli and colleagues found that learning a complex odor proceeded at a faster pace if the animal had previous experience with single components in the complex.[7] If you first train your dog on single scents, he will more rapidly learn complexes that contain those single scents. But a dog trained only on single scents will not always recognize those scents in complex compounds. Dogs must be trained on complex scents in order to become familiar with them.

## Tracking Is Strenuous

Even under normal weather conditions, search work is extremely strenuous for dogs, and they quickly reach their physical limits. Scent-detection work demands high neurological and cerebral activity from dogs. Intensive tracking, for example, requires concentrated muscular movements, in particular because of the peculiar, tensed way of walking and the stretched and bent posture. Tracking's physical demands put an extra load on the joints, and the muscle activity stimulates production of pyruvate and lactate (lactic acid) in the muscular tissue (acidification). Tracking also makes demands on dogs' respiration, heart rate, and body temperature. Dr. Briewasser has researched the effort dogs bring to search work. He tested experienced tracking dogs before and after working out a 1000-pace-long track. Not only did the dogs' body temperature rise considerably, from 100.9 to 104.2°F (38.3–40.1°C),

**Figure 8.8** Intensive tracking requires concentrated muscular movements, in particular because of the peculiar, tensed way of walking and the stretched and bent posture the dog assumes.

but the pulse rate also rose from 92 to 142 beats per minute, and their respiration rate, from 41 to 145 breaths per minute, reached an absolute top level.[8]

In other words, intensive search work requires incredible mental and physical efforts from dogs. If possible, before beginning a search, do warm-up exercises that allow your dog to prepare himself mentally and physically for the task ahead. In his research, Dr. Briewasser also determined that the dog's resting temperature, respiration, and pulse values were reached again only 1.5 hours after tracking was over. This compares to the studies of Blatt, Taylor, and Habal (1972) and Radke (1998). The latter discusses the heat stroke of a pedigreed Malinois working as a police service dog for the Royal Canadian Mounted Police. In this case, the dog's body temperature after a 1312 yard (1200 m) track, followed by bite work with the tracklayer, reached 107.3°F

(41.86°C) and 10 minutes later was still high at 105°F (40.56°C). For these reasons alone, we strongly recommend that you take a relaxing walk with your dog for about five to 10 minutes after search work, and then give him at least 1.5 hours to rest before starting other exercises.

## Dangers of Overheating

It is vitally important for you, the handler, to carefully monitor your dog's health as he works, or even when you are out together in hot weather. Overheating is extremely detrimental to dogs. When the weather is hot, over 82°F (28°C) (especially in high humidity), the dog's body temperature increases a bit, which he tries to prevent by panting. If the temperature increases, the dog's body temperature also increases, in spite of his attempts to cool down in another way (for instance, by lying down on cool pavement). You can help by, first, doing things to decrease his body temperature: bringing your dog into the shade or into a cool room (a cellar, for example), moistening his limbs with cold water, placing icepacks around his head and neck, or carefully sprinkling his body with cold water. If you do not notice your dog's heat control working quickly enough, he will soon develop the clinical symptoms of heat stroke. He will not be able to cool down, and his body temperature will rise to over 104°F (40°C). Because of dilating peripheral capillaries, the total blood vessel volume will increase dramatically, so his circulation will begin to fail. His pulse will become irregular and weak, and he will likely vomit or have diarrhea. He will be exhausted and may pass out.

If your dog's body reaches a temperature of 106.7°F (41.5°C), he is in serious trouble. Cerebral and spinal cord functions become disordered at this point, and your dog will display movement disorders, an increased heart rate, and fast and deep breathing. Unlike panting, this fast, deep breathing is very hard on him.

**Figure 8.9** In temperatures over 82°F (28°C), especially in high humidity, your dog's body temperature increases. He will try to prevent this by panting as much as possible.

**Figure 8.10** Help your dog decrease his body temperature when he is overheated.

Body temperatures of 107.6 to 109.4°F (42–43°C), even endured for a short time, are fatal for dogs. Animals that survive temperatures of 106.7°F (41°C) can suffer permanent cerebral damage and cardiac arrhythmia. Such dogs tire progressively more quickly and weaken in the limbs (particularly the hindquarters). They look like they will faint, and their eyes often roll. Every time such a dog's body heats up again, the dog suffers a blow. In the end, such dogs must be withdrawn from operational service.

## Troubleshooting

It is advantageous to work in a group with other dogs and handlers, and to discuss problems with your colleagues before doing something about them. Others often see things you have not noticed. Discussing and thoroughly analyzing a problem with fellow handlers often leads to a solution. However, even if your dog seems to be healthy and performing well and enjoying the work, you as the handler must be aware of problems that can cause your dog to make mistakes.

## Systematic Mistakes

As discussed in Chapter 2, dogs can learn to react to "systematic" oddities in training and in practice, such as the matching odor in a scent-identification lineup always being collected last in the series, or if the suspect is asked to give odor for a longer period, leading the scent "picture" of the matching odor to be fresher or stronger than the other odors in the lineup. If either of these things are done regularly, the dog learns to react, knowing that choosing a fresh and strong odor leads to a reward. Dutch police-dog handlers are very aware of this danger; precautions are part of the official regulations.

Another systematic mistake that a dog can pick up on is if the odors of the foils are systematically laid out first, and the matching odor is added last. Dogs are sensitive to time and concentration differences. In fact, it appears they find the direction of a track by noticing differences in odor concentration between one footstep and the other. If the matching odor is systematically added to the lineup last, the dog will learn how to interpret this.

One systematic mistake often seen in training detector and SAR dogs involves the dogs always choosing the easiest path to their "find." Instead of really searching for the odor, for example, a lot of search dogs will take the easy way out and just follow the scent of the person who laid out the scent of "victims" in the exercise room or on the training grounds. While this method does lead dogs to the "find," they are not really learning how to search. Instructors of detector and SAR dogs should prevent their pupils from using such footprint highways to come to their goal by having a few people lay tracks in the area to prevent dogs from "cheating."

In training, it is critical to avoid these kinds of systematic mistakes since the dog can and will learn cues from them. These sorts of mistakes can lead you into thinking your dog is working well when he is in fact using quite different cues than the ones you want him to use. A slightly different procedure always brings this error to light, and once you discover the dog has learned to use a different cue from the one you intend, you know you have taken a few steps backward in training.

## Handling Mistakes

When working, dogs must continue to search even if their handlers have given them a verbal correction. If your dog becomes nervous when corrected, he will not proceed to search well but instead will pay attention to you, his handler. The basic trust between you and your dog must be built up together, outside the bounds of search work and training. This makes it possible for you to correct your dog verbally, but only gently and quietly. If your dog reacts strongly to verbal corrections, you may decide to use a thin leash and correct him with a gentle pull instead. If you do this, though, your dog will need to get used to working on a leash during simple search work. This type of correction only works if the dog is completely accustomed to the leash while he is working and is not hindered by it.

## "Shape" and "Content" Problems

Several general training problems can occur when training search dogs. These can be divided roughly into two categories: "shape" and "content." Shape problems are related to the manner (technique) in which search work is performed; content problems are problems with making correct matches.

For example, during search and rescue training, a dog who is not used to walking over rubble will have "shape" problems when the hidden person is in the middle of a rubble pile covered with stones and other material. The dog must be encouraged by her handler to walk over the rubble and then will only have an eye on her handler and won't search. Because of the shape problem, the dog will not be able to find and alert to hidden person, which will result in a content problem.

When you need to solve a shape problem, make recognition (the content) easy for your dog. This means training at a lower level than what your dog is already capable of. In our search and rescue example, we can position the hidden person at the side of the rubble and not cover the person so completely so the dog doesn't have to walk that much over difficult rubble, making it easier for her to be successful.

Training below level will help you work out shape problems for one important reason. When you correct or influence your dog, his attention focuses on you. This means that he will not be paying as much attention to the scent as he should. To prevent an association

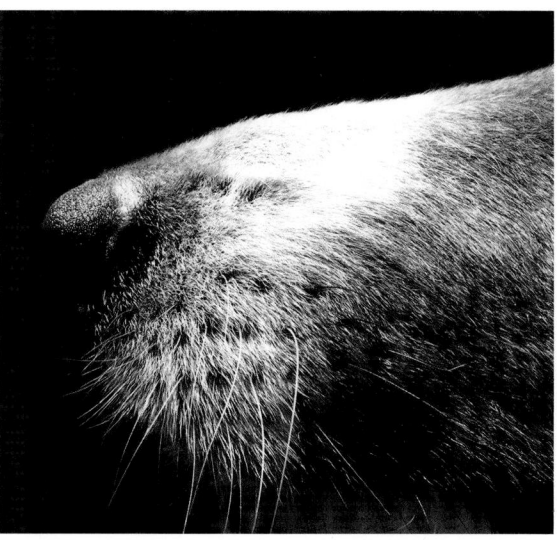

**Figure 8.11** Practice, practice, practice. Regular exposure to training scents leads to physical changes in the olfactory organ that increase the sensitivity for these scents.

between "difficult" scent recognition and handler influence, and to ensure your dog focuses his attention on the scent again as quickly as possible, it is thus important for the work to be easy for him. The reverse is also true: if a dog has content difficulties and cannot make certain recognitions, you should pay less attention to shape elements and reward your dog more quickly than usual, for example.

## Reading the Dog

Handlers must be able to understand their search dogs' behavior, especially the complex and broad range of movements and expressions they engage in while searching. In order to read your dog, it is particularly important to pay attention to all the changes he shows in his behavior. And in order to do that, you have to know your dog well—how he acts in regular circumstances, at home as well as during training. That requires a long and close, cooperative relationship, during which you constantly observe your dog.

During search work, dogs make it clear to their handlers that they have located something by displaying certain behaviors called "alerts": barking, lying down, sitting, and so on. You can also usually know he has found something when he does something unique to him. If your dog has been searching for a while, and if the search has been difficult, his ability to display his "trained alert" may weaken. So it is important that you are able to read your dog's body language, because that language may be the best clue your dog will give you after a long and stressful search. A dog may be indicating, or at least close to finding, the scent he is searching for, if he:

- suddenly changes direction when searching, making a curve, or deviates more or less from a straight line;
- changes his tempo, becoming slower or faster;
- shows interest in a specific area of the search for somewhat longer than normal, even if he is not alerting;
- stands still somewhere, staring at a certain spot, or "pointing" like a hunting dog, standing with one of his legs off the ground and looking;
- begins to scratch or to bite at a particular spot to take away pieces of covering material (if he only scratches once or a few times, he has not ordinarily found the right place. Be careful then and keep quiet, because your dog is still orienting himself.); and
- tries by intentional movements to bring you, the handler, to the scent clue, usually by acting excited and by walking there and back, showing the direction in which to walk.

## Training Advice

It is obvious that we do not know everything there is to know about the sense of smell and that it is impossible to objectively determine what a scent is. Even so it is possible to give a few points of attention to handlers training dogs on scents. The points below are valid for all kinds of scent-detection training.

**Figure 8.12** Performing search work is one of the most enjoyable activities a handler can engage in with his or her dog.

- Check whether your dog is able to perform scent work each time you need him. The physical ability to smell varies, and a dog's motivation to work can also vary. It is sensible to check on your dog's capacity, either shortly before, during, or immediately after a practical case. (Checking after the search may be necessary if there was no time to check before and the search was not successful.)
- Be aware of adaptation (and cross-adaptation). Adaptation may make it impossible for your dog to locate the source of a smell since the environment is already saturated with the smell. Adjust your training and search method and allow your dog to clear his nose.
- Be aware that differences in *amount* of scent can be perceived as differences in *kind* of scent. Train on both small and large amounts of odor, and do not expect immediate success: if your dog can find a small amount it does not automatically mean he will also be able to find a large amount.

- Practice is important, both physically and mentally. Regular exposure to training scents leads to physical changes in the olfactory organ that increase sensitivity to these scents.
- Learning things young makes life easy. Scents learned when young are remembered extremely well. If your dog begins scent training early (perhaps even in the litter), she will be a stronger search dog.
- First train on single scents, then on complexes of scents. This speeds up the learning process.
- It is not always possible to prevent mistakes. The influence of a scent on the behavior of a dog through the limbic system (prompting involuntary, automatic responses), and possible interactions of a scent with memories, can lead to all sorts of unpredictable effects. Try, where possible, to find out why your dog responds in specific ways and then use this information in training.
- Most of the above points are also valid for scent-identification training. However, there is a difference between training for scent-identification lineups and other scent training: in scent-identification lineup training, dogs must continuously match odors and not memorize particular scents. This matching of odors is a far more difficult paradigm than detection, and this in turn has particular consequences for the selection of appropriate dogs.
- It is advantageous to work in a group with other handlers and to discuss problems before doing something about them. Others will often have seen problems you are encountering during training, things you have not noticed. Discussing and thoroughly analyzing a problem with colleagues often leads to a solution.

# 9

# Preventing Investigation Errors

At the beginning of this book, we mention the 2006 appeal case in the Dutch town of Leeuwarden. This appeal sparked an investigation into scent-identification lineups in the Netherlands, because it was lineup-related evidence that helped convict two suspects of a robbery (in the lower court) to 40 and 30 months' imprisonment. In examination in court, the dog handler admitted that he did not always work in accordance with scent-lineup protocol. One rule the handler broke is that scent-identification lineups must be worked out "blind," with the dog handler unaware of where the suspect's odors have been placed on the scent platform.

Breaking this rule could only happen if the certified police helper, who prepares the scent lineup, was also complicit. To avoid mistakes, the helper first writes the placement scheme of the different tubes on a white board—the rules state that the helper must wipe this scheme off the white board before the dog handler enters the room, to prevent the handler from knowing what scents are where.

The court could do nothing else but exclude the evidence gathered from the scent-identification lineup, and because there was almost no other evidence, the suspects were acquitted. Immediately after that, the National Department of Criminal Investigation started an investigation into both police officers. Both had

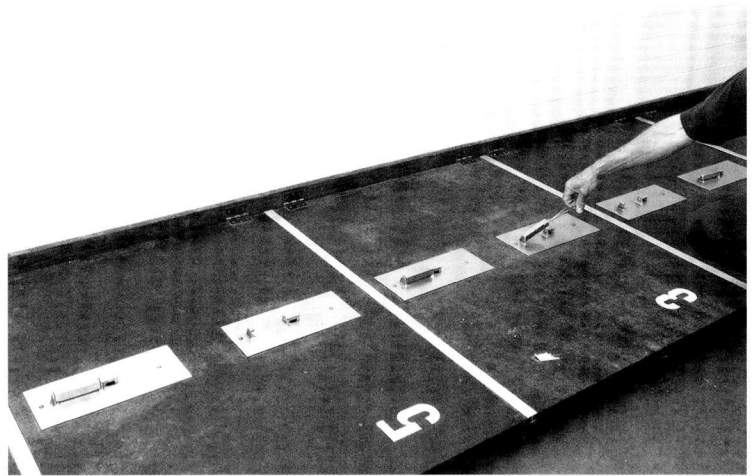

**Figure 9.1** In the Netherlands, a certified helper places the stainless-steel scent carriers on the lineup platforms. The handler is not in the room. (KLPD, 2002)

testified in the official report of the scent lineups in question that "the dog handler wasn't acquainted with the positions of the tubes on the platform," and both of them signed this report. This false testimony could have been easily avoided had they worked carefully and stuck to the protocol. Videotaping the process, and having another controller in the room, may also help maintain quality control of scent lineups.

   In this chapter, we talk about how to avoid and prevent investigation errors. We will do this by discussing the different causes of such errors, including:

1. Unintentional errors
2. Fraud
3. Use of civilians in criminal investigations
4. Contaminated scents
5. Improper training
6. Not understanding the human influence on dogs.

## 1. Unintentional Errors

### SLOPPY WORK

Sloppy and hasty installation and investigation of scent lineups naturally leads to errors. To begin, the helper must carefully install the scent carriers into the platform, working according to protocol. He or she must follow the correct sequence scheme worked out on the white board; then that white board must be erased. Then, once the lineup is ready, the handlers and dogs must also work carefully. Handlers must take care not to put pressure on their dogs, or push them to speed along.

We often see undue pressure on the tracking dog following scent traces in human footprints. Mistakes can also occur on the track when people are careless and contaminate scents and footprints. Contamination can happen easily in mantrailing, when the *corpus delicti* is given to the dog.

As soon as people slacken their attention to the rules, mistakes occur. If handlers and helpers do not work according to protocol, the suspect's defense attorney will naturally demand exclusion of any information gathered that is related to scent identification.

### MANAGEMENT ATTENTION

Managers of scent-identification units need to be aware of the pitfalls that occur from evaluating units by the number of positive identifications "scored." It is essential that whoever manages the unit focuses on the right parameters for evaluation. The focus should be on quality, not quantity.

Looking at the percentage of operational lineups where a dog has made a positive identification has limited value in detecting errors. However, if, within a group of dogs that all perform the same kind of lineups, a certain dog performs worse than the other dogs, this may be something to look at more closely. It may mean that this dog requires more training. Some insight can be gained

**Figure 9.2** Management should focus on controllable quality parameters for their dog handlers.

if you present this dog with copies of lineups that other dogs correctly worked out.

But comparing the percentage of positive identifications between dogs that work in geographically different areas, and thus with materials and suspects collected by different police investigative teams, does not necessarily say much about a difference in quality of the dogs involved. Perhaps the individual police teams have different attitudes toward scent-identification lineups, one team requesting them to support the admission of a suspect, and the other team seeing them as a last resort when everything else has failed. The areas in which the dogs work could also differ in the quality of the scent traces collected and stored.

Management should not focus on positive identifications as a quality parameter, and they certainly should not demonstrate enthusiasm for a high percentage of "positive identifications." This is potentially dangerous for the reliability of the lineups.

Management should also be careful when assessing the scent-identification teams regarding the number of cases in which dogs are being used. While perfectly sensible to do this in areas where scent identification has proven itself, in cases where scent identification is not yet an accepted tool, and where the team has little opportunity to show their work, such a focus may encourage the team to accept poor quality scent traces for investigation. One can expect a no-recognition in such cases, which will not help promote the acceptance of scent-identification lineups.

Management should focus on controllable quality parameters: the percentage of recognitions in control trials, which should be as high as possible, and the percentage of mistakes (instead of non-recognitions), which should be as low as possible. All dogs, of course, make mistakes, so perfection is not possible. However, if the number of successful recognitions reaches impossible heights, managers should take a careful look at why that might be.

By analyzing the procedures followed in conducting lineups, improvements can be made to procedures or to the information given to all relevant parties. For example, we now see that the courts are paying more attention to the correct collection and registration of scent traces. Too often, the official documentation about this part of the process lacks the necessary detail. By informing the police officers involved about correct procedure, this mistake can be adjusted before it leads to the devaluation of scent-identification lineups as a whole.

It follows that managers have a duty to inform the judicial system about the relevance and reliability of scent-identification lineups. Everyone in the system needs to be aware of what a scent-identification lineup is: establishing, with a certain amount of reliability, an odor link between an object and a suspect. They also need to know that there are regulations to be met, and how to check these. They need to realize that this odor link is part of a chain of evidence: the scent object itself needs to be linked to the crime.

All police officers in contact with judicial members about scent lineups need to follow a professional approach and accept the limitations of what dogs can do. Claiming, "My dog never makes a mistake," for example, discredits the speaker as a serious professional, since everyone knows this is impossible.

## 2. Fraud

In some fraud cases, suspects have paid dog handlers for a certain result, but causes of other frauds vary widely. For example, if under too much pressure to get results at work, dog handlers may try to solve a case quickly without worrying about the truth. Other dog handlers may try to disguise the poor quality of a dog or his training by "improving" dog's performance through influence.

Some dog handlers get overly attached to their reputation. The media are always looking over the shoulders of criminal investigators, and the performances of handlers and dogs are often featured in the press and on television. Some people are attracted to this brand of stardom and will try to "solve" as many cases as possible with their dogs to augment their fame.

Among the members of a team of dog handlers, there may be keen but sound competition regarding who has the best-trained dog. However, this competition can become unhealthy if one dog handler is tempted to commit fraud in order to outperform teammates.

A proper quality-control system, such as videotaping the performances of dogs and handlers, may detect fraud over the course of time. Did the teams follow the protocol to the letter? Are departures from accepted process mentioned in the official report of the case? Such questions and a regular review of process can help prevent or uncover fraudulent dog handling.

## AN EXPLOSIVE CASE

One case of outright fraud was revealed in 2003 in the state of Virginia. D.A. Smith writes about this case in "Fraudulent Use of Canines in Police Work." Russell Ebersole, a dog trainer from Stephenson near Winchester, had a dog-training business called Detector Dogs Against Drugs and Explosives. He received $700,000 to train 23 explosive detector dogs for the U.S. government. The dogs guarded numerous government buildings in and around Washington, DC. However, he was exposed as a fraud after a government agent tested his dogs. Two cars were driven through checkpoints of buildings Eberdole's dogs were guarding: one car had 50 pounds (over 20 kg) of dynamite and another car had 50 pounds of plastic explosives. None of the 23 dogs found the explosives. The dogs' inability to detect the explosives was investigated—it turns out Ebersole had faked the dogs' certifications and lied about the handlers' training. He was arrested for 26 cases of fraud and forgery and eventually was convicted and sentenced to 18 years in prison. He was ordered to repay $700,000 to the government.

## 3. Use of Civilians in Criminal Investigations

We find it odd that civilian dog handlers think they can help a criminal investigation. We have never seen civilians searching for blood traces, fingerprints, DNA, cartridges, or weapons at a crime scene, thinking they can do better than the forensic investigators. But as soon as the police employ search dogs, or even actively decide not to use search dogs for technical reasons (for instance, the tracks or traces might be too old), civilians emerge with their dogs and want to involve themselves in the investigation. This happens especially in cases of missing persons. When the police exclude civilians from an area because they suspect a crime was committed, some dog handlers will even contact the families of missing persons and offer their help. Some do not hesitate to criticize the police in the media for not accepting their help.

**Figure 9.3** We never see civilians arrive at a crime scene insisting that they be allowed to search for blood traces, fingerprints, DNA, cartridges, or weapons, yet civilian dog handlers will often want to involve themselves in a case.

If civilians and their SAR, tracking, or mantrailing dogs are used in investigations, they must meet the same standards as are used for police K9s, and they should be able to demonstrate this with certifications showing they have passed the correct examinations. Suspect (homegrown) programs and examinations should be strictly guarded against.

## "MISSING" CAN BECOME A CRIME

Many missing persons cases evolve into criminal cases. In such instances, civilians and their dogs must withdraw from the scene and leave the case to forensic investigators. This can be difficult because the civilians do not want to give up searching, do not want to leave the search area, and so they thwart police work. In these situations, it is sometimes necessary for police officers to intervene and deny civilians access to the site.

Some SAR groups, such as civilians with trackers or mantrailers, walk into areas of police concern like bulls in a china shop, without concerning themselves that a crime may have been committed. In training, such civilian dog handlers should learn how to recognize the signs that a crime could have taken place, and then how to properly notify authorities and withdraw from the area.

**Figure 9.4** Be very careful when using civilians for police tasks or when civilians are around during missing-persons cases.

## SUSPECT EVIDENCE

On September 13, 2003, 11-year-old Shakira Johnson left her family's home in Cleveland, Ohio, and went to a party. She never showed up. On October 15, after an anonymous tip, the police found her partly decomposed nude body in a weed-strewn field about a mile and a half (2.4 km) from her house. The inquest proved that on the day she disappeared she was sexually assaulted and killed. Soon, Daniel Hines, 26, a learning-disabled handyman from Cleveland, was suspected and arrested. Hines had recently been released on bail after a sexual assault charge involving his cousin.

More than 30 days after Johnson disappeared, the FBI asked for the assistance of a bloodhound. The dog found a "track" where the body was discovered, and he followed it, but soon lost it. The bloodhound "scented" Johnson's odor in two other locations: first, in the bathroom of a house Hines shared with his family (a place where a lot of people had been in and out), and second, at the

**Figure 9.5** More than 30 days after Shakira Johnson vanished, the FBI asked for the assistance of a bloodhound.

passenger side door of Hines's van, which was stored at a police impound lot. The strange thing about this is that a police report showed the police had used two dogs to investigate the van one month earlier, and the result was "negative." After the two dogs found no scent, police returned the van, only seizing it again later for the bloodhound.

In this case, the judge ruled that the dog handler would not be allowed to testify because there were no eyewitnesses who could corroborate that Johnson had been in Hines's van or home. Hines's attorneys argued that the dog handler's testimony was unreliable, and on December 19, 2004, the seven women and five men of the jury acquitted Daniel Hines of kidnapping and murdering Shakira Johnson.

## 4. Contaminated Scents

### DUAL-PURPOSE DOGS

Here "dual purpose" means dogs trained for detecting human odor as well as drugs or explosives. A dual-purpose dog used in a scent lineup may alert to the wrong scent. Remember the Fitting-Room Murder Case from the first chapter of this book? Police dog Tim investigated the scent lineup in that case, but he was also a drug detector dog. The bicycle dealer suspect in the lineup was indicated by Tim, perhaps because he was a drug user.

### PRESERVE SCENTED OBJECTS PROPERLY

Odors important to a case need to be preserved correctly, uncontaminated by other scents. And when offering scent to the dog, we must be careful not to let one scented object come into contact with another. Those in charge of scented objects must follow correct cleaning procedures when dealing with tubes and glass jars: they should be either sterilized in a stove or first washed with soap in a dishwasher dedicated to that task and then boiled in clean water.

## CLEAN-SCENT TRAINING

If we want a dog to be interested in a certain scent, in training we always offer the purest possible form of that scent in the right quantity. In lineups or when starting a dog mantrailing, the dog should receive only the pure, uncontaminated scent of the suspect (or whoever was walking the trail). After every training session, those articles should be cleaned thoroughly.[1]

## MAKING THE IMPOSSIBLE POSSIBLE

We have nothing against bloodhounds or working with bloodhounds. In both the U.S. and Europe, there are many good and honest, hardworking search-dog handlers that know their dogs' limits in terms of scent perception, and they will not expect more than what is possible from those dogs. If a limitation presents itself on the job—for example, if the scent is too old—these handlers will accept that and move on.

What we object to are those search-dog handlers who sometimes unintentionally, even intentionally, try to make the impossible possible. Where honest dog handlers stop, these dog handlers go on, committing fraud in the process. In this way, they discredit honest search-dog handlers. All they want is to be right and "steal the show" with their dogs.

But there is more! Many good search-dog handlers are criticized by their superiors or civil servants because their dogs cannot perform the things such fraudulent handlers say *their* dogs can do. The superiors hear or read these spectacular results and ask their dog handlers, "Why can't our dogs do such things?"

Well, we hope we have shown that no dog can perform the impossible. Following are some tips for managers of dog handlers from D.A. Smith:

- First of all, check the backgrounds and certifications of all handlers and dogs. Ask for certification from a national police dog association.

**Figure 9.6** Many good police-dog handlers are criticized by their superiors because their dogs cannot do the things fraudulent handlers say their dogs can do.

- Be very careful with claims that a dog can do something other police dogs cannot.
- Be cautious using civilians for police tasks; check the backgrounds and certifications of all civilian handlers and dogs. Be sure the certifications and judges of the exams are up to the same standards of those used for police dogs. In missing persons cases, be careful using civilians who are not trained in recognizing the signs of a crime. Remember that most civilians are not trained in evidence preservation or court testimony.

## 5. Improper Training

### EASY SCORING BY FOLLOWING TRACKS

Be aware that dogs will always choose the easiest way to come to their "find." Know that if there is only one scent trail in the area, dogs will follow it, knowing that the trail likely belongs to the person who prepared the scent articles for them to investigate. Instructors of detector and SAR dogs should stop dogs from using such "footprint highways" to come to their goals by having many different people lay tracks (not always leading to the find) in the room or area to be investigated.

## SELECTION BEFORE TRAINING

Training can lead to success only if the starting material is good. We have to look carefully at the characteristics of the dogs we want to train. And it is equally important to look at the characteristics of the handlers who are going to teach the dogs, and to look at the kind of teams the dogs and handlers make. Scent training is mentally the most challenging kind of training. It requires a stable, mature mentality in both the dog and the handler.

Of course, the dog must be healthy, too. Many kinds of illnesses and medications affect the dog's nose. Training a dog whose sense of smell is not optimal will lead to all kinds of unnecessary, stressful situations that are detrimental to training. The physical characteristics of trainable dogs are:

- completely healthy and sound in life and limb;
- easy and fast movements;
- strong and muscled bodies;
- good sense of smell, sight, and hearing;
- strong and powerful mouths;
- optimal physical condition and great stamina;
- strong legs, and feet with strong soles;
- adapted to the weather and climate in which they must work;
- coats suitable for work.

The mental characteristics of potentially good scent-detection dogs include:

- placid composure (self-confident, stable, not nervous or afraid);
- lively, interested temperament;
- willingness to continue working even if there is no immediate reward;

- high practical intelligence and good adaptive intelligence. We distinguish between three forms of intelligence, namely the instinctive, the practical, and the adaptive. By *instinctive intelligence* we mean all hereditary skills and behavior. For instance, the hunting drive: every puppy runs after a moving object. By *practical intelligence* we mean the speed with which, and the degree to which, the dog conforms to the desires of the handler: roughly said, how quickly and how correctly the dog learns the different exercises. *Adaptive intelligence* can be divided into two abilities: learning proficiency, which means how quickly the dog develops adequate behavior in new situations, and problem-solving ability. This last is the dog's ability to choose the correct behavior with which to solve a problem.
- a natural ability to use the nose to find objects;
- a not too high prey drive: if the dog defends rewards too strongly, she will be focused on the reward itself too much, which might prevent her from searching well;
- high bring drive: by retrieving her reward to the handler, the dog shares it, which is good for the team;
- ability to cope with mistakes: if corrected (a verbal correction should be sufficient), the dog should remain composed, willing to work, and not lose the desire to search and retrieve. Dogs that cannot cope quickly with being corrected are very difficult to work with.

These characteristics are found only in mature dogs. Although training can begin before puberty, we have not found that early training significantly shortens the training time or increases the final performance level. Instead, prepare your dog for scent tasks by ensuring she is well socialized, generally obedient, and interested in searching (play search and retrieve games). Here, care should be taken that the dog learns to search with her nose—active use of the nose enhances its development, ensuring a good starting point for scent training when the time comes.

## THE TEAM: HANDLER AND DOG

Some of your dog's characteristics develop during training and cannot be fully tested before training begins. You can try to test your dog's will to work before and during training, for example, but the final test comes in the field, when your dog must maintain the will to work while performing special scent tasks. A dog's ability to cope with mistakes is another characteristic you cannot really test beforehand, important as it is.

Dog handlers must themselves have stable characters and not be easily agitated by their dogs' behavior. They must know how to interpret the behavior of different dogs and be able to read their signals quickly. They must have a lot of patience, be willing to review their own training critically, and (for the sake of the dog) regularly go a step back in training. They must be aware of the possible pitfalls they can come across in this work, especially the Clever Hans kind of problems. This means that they must accept that it is good if their dogs do not pay very much attention to them, which is quite different from normal obedience work. Dog handlers must realize that dogs are the only ones who can smell well enough to solve the problems the team encounters. They must never try to force their dogs into "alerting a scent clue," but instead try to adapt the training to maneuver their dogs into understanding what is expected of them. In short, dog handlers must be intelligent and sensitive trainers who always stay one step ahead of their dogs.

Inadequate handlers can ruin potentially good dogs. Good handlers can go quite a long way with not-so-good dogs, but they will not be able to achieve the high standard necessary for operational work. In the end, it is best for managers and handler peers to look first at the handler critically, and if things do not go well, stop. Dog handlers should like their dogs, and there should be no tension between them, neither during training nor outside of training. In fact, outside of training, handlers and their dogs should continue to improve their relationships. If there is stress between handler and dog, it will show up in scent training and play a negative role.

## MATCH THE DOG AND TRAINING METHOD

Good selection practices can prevent the possibility of starting out an unsuitable dog in training. Sometimes, however, a dog may be fit, but not "fit" the only training method to which the handler or instructor subscribes.

A good dog handler (and instructor) should know several training methods and be well informed about new developments in dog training. This is the only way handlers and instructors can adapt training methods to their dogs in order to get the best results. Every dog is unique and needs a certain way of training. We are always surprised when we discover handlers or instructors who only know one method of training and try to fit all dogs into that method. The dog, then, must adapt to the method, instead of vice versa, and the results are usually not up to the mark.

## UNDER PRESSURE FOR RESULTS

If you try to train search dogs to perform a task in too little time, the dogs will learn the exercises under pressure and negative stress. Just like people, dogs need time to process new exercises or circumstances. This kind of rushing happens as a matter of course, but we have also known dog handlers to rush through training in order to have more free time for themselves.

## GOOD PHYSICAL, MENTAL, AND "SEARCH" CONDITION

The dog's physical, mental, and "search" conditions influence the dog's achievements.

The dog can be said to be in good physical condition if his muscles are supple and well trained, and his body is in an optimal state. Dogs should always be fed properly, or they will experience physical exhaustion after brief exertion. When dogs are hungry, they lack concentration and have insufficient energy to perform, as well as intense nervousness.

Dogs can be said to have fine mental status when they independently and enthusiastically work out their exercises without their handlers applying pressure or compulsion. When fine mental status is lacking, we see apathy, stress, or physical tiredness.

The dog's "search" condition is the ability to concentrate long enough to get through the scent work. When lacking, we see dogs that need a break after a short time because they do not have the mental stamina to continue.

### HIGH EXAMINATION REQUIREMENTS

The examination requirements for service dogs are set high so their professional work can be guaranteed. In the highest examinations for sport tracking, dogs need to work out three-hour-old tracks of 5250 feet (1600 m), and in mantrailing they must investigate much longer and older trails. So we were astonished when we discovered a North American test for police search dogs that required only a one-hour-old track of about 3181 feet (1000 m).

**Figure 9.7** SAR dog handlers should be able to recognize the signs that indicate a crime could have taken place in missing-persons cases.

## INSURANCE FRAUD

Deceit involving police dogs can take many forms. A special case of fraud with a police dog came to light in November 2009. In Oakland, about 31 miles (50 km) from Memphis, Tennessee, a case of insurance fraud with a police dog came to court. Former Oakland police chief, Bob Tisdale, and two former Oakland officers, Herbert Brewer and Billy Allen Usselton, were indicted on charges of faking the death of a police dog named Kit in 2004, then collecting the $5000 insurance policy for the town. Kit was reportedly killed during training in Hardeman County. Four years later, authorities received information that the dog was alive, leading to an inquiry by the Tennessee Bureau of Investigations, which later announced Kit was found living in Tipton County. Tisdale pleaded guilty, got three years' probation and had to pay $1,666.66 in restitution (his share after the amount was split three ways).

## 6. Lack of Familiarity with Human Influence on Dogs

As we have noted throughout this book, dogs easily and quickly learn to react to even minor, unconscious cues—the Clever Hans cues. It is important to know about the influence you exert on a dog as a handler—or as an instructor, helper, or spectator. Dogs quickly learn to react to the people around them who know where something or someone is hidden. They will look toward the instructors and watch their intentional gestures and also their unintentional ones to figure out when they are close to finding what they are supposed to find. Stepping aside slightly, stopping a conversation, holding of breath—all of these signs tell dogs exactly what they need to know. The only way to avoid such Clever Hans cues is, as soon as the dog understands the technique of tracking or searching, to work "blind" and not know the position of the track or the hiding place.

### CONTROLLED OR TRULY BLIND?

A lot of dog handlers think they track blind because they do not know the path of the track. But the tracklayers or instructors, who do know the track, walk close behind the dog handler, who trusts that the tracklayer will interfere if things go wrong. In this scenario, after working out a few tracks, dogs will learn to listen to the tracklayer's footsteps, voice, and breathing. So this is not blind tracking but "controlled" tracking.

Working blind means being there with your dog, all alone, with nobody in the neighborhood who knows the path of the track and so can influence the tracking. In truly blind tracking, the dog handler knows nothing, except the place where he or she has to start the dog (near a tree, car, footprint, and so on), and proceeds with the dog to work it out, then comes back with the articles found along the track and/or the tracklayer who was sitting or lying at the end of the track.

This difference between controlled and blind working can also be seen in the exercises detector dogs work out as they learn to search for drugs, explosives, and arson, or in SAR dogs that must

**Figure 9.8** Truly blind tracking involves the dog and handler working on a track all alone, with nobody around who might know the path of the track, so nobody who can influence the dog's tracking.

learn to search for people trapped beneath rubble. In these cases, there is a helper present who has hidden the substances or people and, just like the instructor on the track, stays in the room the dog has to search. Most of the time, these helpers face the hiding place. Dogs learn unerringly to conduct their searches in the vicinity of these people because they have noted that helpers and instructors always want to see the dogs' alert.

If the handler and dog are too far away from the hiding place, they normally can tell just by looking at the position or the attention of the helper and/or instructor. If the helper or instructor suddenly stops talking, for example, the handler may conclude that he or she and the dog have neared the right spot. So, this situation, too, represents a kind of controlled searching.

Truly blind searching in training happens only if the helper or instructor indicates several rooms, objects, or buildings in which the handler and dog may find something, and then the team must work alone and bring the find to the instructor. Only in such a situation will the handler be able to show he or she can work alongside the dog, together as a team. Only then is the search exercise the exciting and realistic preparation needed for success in the field.

# Notes

## NOTES TO SCENT-IDENTIFICATION LINEUPS

1 On April 22, 2008, the Prosecutor's Office at the Supreme Court transacted a procedure in the field of criminal law. The case number is 07/10591, ECLI code: NL: PHR: 2008: BC9637. Before 2008, the statement was filed as National Case Law Number (LJN) BC9637.

2 F. Schmidt, *Verbrecherspur und Polizeihund* (Augsburg: Selbstverlag SV, 1910), 70–71. Translation by the authors.

3 F. Schmidt, *Polizeihund-Erfolge und Neue Winke* (Augsburg: Selbstverlag SV, 1911), 120–121. Translation by the authors.

4 J. Water, *De grote daden van politiehond "Albert"* (Amsterdam: De Courant-Nieuws van de Dag, 1948), 12. Translation by the authors.

5 F.J.J. Buytendijk, *De psychologie van den hond* (Amsterdam: Kosmos, 1932), 83–84.

6 J. Water, *De grote daden van politiehond "Albert"* (Amsterdam: De Courant-Nieuws van de Dag, 1948), 25. Translation by the authors.

7 J. Water, *De grote daden van politiehond "Albert"* (Amsterdam: De Courant-Nieuws van de Dag, 1948), 11–12. Translation by the authors.

8 Ph. v.d. Most, "Diensthonden en Dressuur," *De Hond* no. 11 (May 9, 1930), 399–400. Translation by the authors.

9 F.J.J. Buytendijk, *De psychologie van den hond* (Amsterdam: Kosmos, 1932) 85–86. Translation by the authors.

10 The Deventer murder case's file number in the Dutch Supreme Court is 22-02-2005, LJN AR5714. Read more about this case on Wikipedia.

11 See Ed Lavandera, "Dogs Sniff Out Wrong Suspect; Scent Lineups Questioned," CNN, October 5, 2009, accessed February 15, 2015, CNN.com/crime. See also Innocence Project of Texas, "Dog Scent Lineups, A Junk Science Injustice," A Special Report by the Innocence Project of Texas, September 21, 2009, accessed February 15, 2015, http://ipoftexas.org.

12 See Ed Lavandera, "Dogs Sniff Out Wrong Suspect; Scent Lineups Questioned," CNN, October 5, 2009, accessed February 15, 2015, CNN.com/crime.

13  Innocence Project of Texas, "Dog Scent Lineups, A Junk Science Injustice," A Special Report by the Innocence Project of Texas, September 21, 2009, accessed February 15, 2015, http://ipoftexas.org.

14  A.E. Taslitz, "Does the Cold Nose Know? The Unscientific Myth of the Dog Scent Lineup" *The Hastings Law Journal* 42 (1990): 15–134.

15  J. Wójcikiewicz, *Scientific Evidence in Judicial Proceedings* (Kraków: Institute of Forensic Research Publishers, 2000).

16  S. Marchal, O. Bregeras, D. Puaux, R. Gervais, and B. Ferry, "Rigorous Training of Dogs Leads to High Accuracy in Human Scent Matching-To-Sample Performance," *PLoS ONE* 11, no. 2 (2016): e0146963. DOI: 10.1371/journal.pone.0146963.

17  A. Schoon and R. Haak, *K9 Suspect Discrimination* (Calgary: Detselig Enterprises/ Brush Education, 2002).

## NOTES TO DOGS' RESPONSIVENESS TO HUMAN GESTURES

1  O. Pfungst, *Clever Hans: The Horse of Mr. Von Osten* (New York: Holt, Rinehart & Winston, 1911), 262.

2  K. Krall, *Denkende Tiere, Beitrage zur Tierseelenkunde auf Grund eigener Versuche, der Kluge Hans und meine Pferde Muhamed und Zarif* (Leipzig: Friedrich Engelman, 1912).

3  A. Miklősi, R. Polgárdi, J. Topál, and V. Csányi, "Use of Experimenter-Given Cues in Dogs," *Animal Cognition* 1, no. 2 (1998): 113–121.

4  M.W. Fox, "A Comparative Study of Development of Facial Expressions in Canids: Wolf, Coyote and Foxes," *Behaviour* 36 (1970): 49–73.

5  K. Soproni, A. Miklősi, J. Topál, and V. Csányi. "Comprehension of Human Communicative Signs in Pet Dogs (*Canis familiaris*)," *Journal of Comparative Psychology* 115, no. 2 (June 2001): 122–126.

6  K. Soproni, A. Miklősi, J. Topál, and V. Csányi, "Dogs' (*Canis familaris*) Responsiveness to Human Pointing Gestures," *Journal of Comparative Psychology* 116, no. 1 (2002): 27–34.

7  P. Pongrácz, A. Miklősi, E. Kubinyi, K. Gurobi, J. Topál, and V. Csányi, "Social Learning in Dogs: The Effect of a Human Demonstrator on the Performance of Dogs in a Detour Task," *Animal Behaviour* 62, no. 6 (2001): 1109–1117.

## NOTES TO TRACKING DOGS IN CRIME INVESTIGATION

1  B.P. Grenfell and A.S. Hunt, eds., *The Oxyrhynchus Papyri: Part IX* (London, 1912), 31.

2  H. Mynsinger, "1473. *Puoch von den valken, habichten, sperbern, pfaeriden, und hunden*," in *Der deutsche Schäferhund in Wort und Bild* ed. M. von Stephanitz (Jena: Anton Kampfe). Translation by the authors.

3  M. Siber, *Die Hunde Afrikas* (St. Gallen, 1899), 81. Translation by the authors.

4  M. von Stephanitz, *The German Shepherd Dog/Verein für deutsche Schäferhunde* (SV), 8th edition (Augsburg: 1950), 442–443. Translation by the authors.

5  L. Huyghebaert, "Onze Belgische rashonden," *Cultura* (Antwerp) (1925): 3229–3230. Translation by the authors.

6  Ibid., 3295.

7  L. van der Snickt, "Programme dressage des chiens," *Chasse et Pêche* (Brussels) (June 12, 1898): 22. Translation by the authors.

8   F. Schmidt, *Polizeihund-Erfolge und Neue Winke* (Augsburg: Selbstverlag SV, 1911), 134. Translation by the authors.

9   Ibid., 142.

10  Ibid.

11  Ibid., 66.

12  Ibid.

13  Ibid., 126.

14  Ibid., 130.

15  Ibid., 130–131.

16  Ibid., 131–132.

17  Ibid., 57.

18  Ibid., 155.

19  Ibid., 161.

20  Ibid., 121.

21  J. Hansmann, "Unter welchen Gesichtspunkten erfolgt die praktische Verwendung des Polizeifährtenhundes?" *Zeitschrift für Hundeforschung* I (1931): 14–30. Translation by the authors.

22  J. Water, *De grote daden van politiehond "Albert"* (Amsterdam: De Courant-Nieuws van de Dag, 1948), 9–10. Translation by the authors.

23  Ibid., 10.

24  M. Soschtschenko, "The Remarkable Nose in a Police Dog," *De Hond* 4 (1929): 87–88. Translation by the authors.

25  K. Most, "Neue Versuche über Spürfähigkeit," *Z.D. Hund*, 18 (1926): 31–35. J. Hansmann, "Unter welchen Gesichtspunkten erfolgt die praktische Verwendung des Polizeifährtenhundes?" *Zeitschrift für Hundeforschung* I (1931): 14–30.

26  R. Gerritsen and R. Haak, *K9 Professional Tracking: A Complete Manual for Theory and Training* (Calgary: Detselig Enterprises Ltd., 2001).

27  R.S. Moxley, "The Case of the Dog That Couldn't Sniff Straight," *OC Weekly* (November 5, 2005), http://www.ocweekly.com/news/the-case-of-the-dog-that-couldnt-sniff-straight-6376132.

28  Innocence Project, "James Ochoa: 1 Year in Prison, Innocent," accessed January 15, 2016, http://www.innocenceproject.org/cases-false-imprisonment/james-ochoa.

29  Ibid.

30  Ibid.

31  Ibid.

32  R.S. Moxley, "The Case of the Dog That Couldn't Sniff Straight," *OC Weekly* (November 5, 2005). http://www.ocweekly.com/news/the-case-of-the-dog-that-couldnt-sniff-straight-6376132.

33  Ibid.

34  Ibid.

35  Innocence Project, "James Ochoa: 1 Year in Prison, Innocent," accessed January 15, 2016, http://www.innocenceproject.org/cases-false-imprisonment/james-ochoa.

36  D. Katz, 1937. *Animals and Men*. Longmans, Green & Co., London.

37 Innocence Project of Florida, "*Florida Today* Blows Open John Preston Story," *Plain Error* (blog), June 22, 2009, http://floridainnocence.org/content/?p=899.

38 *Florida Today*, "K9 Con Man John Preston Cases: Innocent Jailed, Scandal Blooms Again," June 26, 2009. See also *Florida Today*, "K9 Con Man John Preston: The Geraldo Rivera Debunking," June 27, 2009.

## NOTES TO SCENT RESEARCH AND TRACKING EXPERIMENTS

1  J. Von Uexküll and G. Kriszat. *Streifzüge durch die Umwelten von Tieren and Menschen* (Berlin: Verständliche Wissenschaft, XXI, 1934), 5-7. Authors translation.

2  G.J. Romanes, "Experiments on the Sense of Smell in Dogs," *Nature* 36, no. 925 (1887): 273-274. http://dx.doi.org/10.1038/036273a0.

3  F. Schmidt, *Verbrecherspur und Polizeihund* (Augsburg: Selbstverlag SV, 1910).

4  P. Böttger, "Hunde im Dienste der Kriminalpolizei," *Zeitschrift für Hundeforschung* 5 (1937): 10.

5  K. Most, and G.H. Brückner, "Über Voraussetzungen und den derzeitigen Stand der Nasenleistungen von Hunden," *Zeitschrift für Hundeforschung* 5 (1936): 9-30.

6  F.J.J. Buytendijk, *De psychologie van den hond* (Amsterdam: Kosmos, 1932), 92.

7  J. Hansmann, "Unter welchen Gesichtspunkten erfolgt die praktische Verwendung des Polizeifährtenhundes?" *Zeitschrift für Hundeforschung* I (1931): 14-30.

8  R. Belleville, "Neue Versuche auf dem Gebiet der Fährtenarbeit und des Identifizierens von Gegenständen auf der Fährte," *Zeitschrift für Hundeforschung* XIII (1938): 17-28.

9  T. Uchida, *Proceedings from the International Congress of Zoology* (XIV), Copenhagen (1953): 292.

10  J. Honhon, "L'Olfaction chez le Chien: Son rôle dans le pistage et la localisation d'une source odorante" (Diss., Paris, 1967).

11  K. Zuschneid, "Die Riechleistung des Hundes" (PhD diss., Freie University, Berlin, 1973).

12  W. Neuhaus, "Die Bedeutung des Schnüffelns für das Riechen des Hundes," *Zeitung für Säugetierkunde* 46 (1981): 301-310.

13  A. Thesen, J.B. Steen, and K.B. Døving, "Behaviour of Dogs during Olfactory Tracking," *Journal of Experimental Biology* 180 (1993): 247-251.

## NOTES TO ERRORS IN MANTRAILING

1  J. O'Malley, "Wade's Attorney Tries to Discredit Bloodhounds' Work," *Anchorage Daily News*, August 29, 2008, 1.

2  M. Miller and D. Klaidman, "Hunt for the Anthrax Killer," *Newsweek*, August 12, 2002, 23-27.

3  Ibid.

4  C. Johnson, D.Q. Wilber, and D. Eggen, "Government Asserts Ivins Acted Alone," *The Washington Post*, August 7, 2008.

5  D. Wright, D. Gentile, and C. Montgomery, "Heroic Tracking Dogs Prove Scott Lied to Police," *National Enquirer*, January 6, 2004.

6  L. Stambler, "Peterson Trial: Dog Tracked Laci's Scent," *People Magazine*, January 9, 2004.

7  S. Ritea, "Dogs to Aid Search for B.R. Serial Killer," *The Times-Picayune*, September 21, 2002.

8  Ibid.

9  T. Fields-Meyer, "Bones of Contention: The Owner of a Crime-Solving Superdog Stands Charged with Planting Evidence," *People Magazine* 60, no. 20 (November 17, 2003).

10  D.A. Smith, "Fraudulent Use of Canines in Police Work" (Ypsilanti, MI: Eastern Michigan University, School of Police Staff and Command, 2004), 7–8.

11  R. Furst, "Bloodhound Handler's Credentials Questioned in Search for Missing Men," *Minneapolis Star Tribune*, January 5, 2003.

12  Ibid, 11.

13  T. Langford, "Child Protection Official's Death Haunts Victoria County," *Houston Chronicle*, July 3, 2006.

14  R. Casey, "Dog's Nose Fallible as a Crime Lab," *Houston Chronicle*, June 30, 2009.

15  Ibid.

16  Innocence Project, "Know the Cases and Invalidated or Improper Forensic Science," 2009, accessed January 15, 2016, http://www.innocenceproject.org.

17  See A. Schoon and R. Haak, *K9 Suspect Discrimination: Training and Practicing Scent Identification Lineups* (Calgary, Canada: Detselig Enterprises Ltd., 2002).

18  R. Furst, "Bloodhound Handler's Credentials Questioned in Search for Missing Men," *Minneapolis Star Tribune*, January 5, 2003.

19  Associated Press, "Families, Police Clash on Use of Bloodhound," January 8, 2003.

20  R. Furst, "Bloodhound Handler's Credentials Questioned in Search for Missing Men," *Minneapolis Star Tribune*, January 5, 2003.

21  J. O'Malley, "Defense Challenges Reliability of Bloodhounds' Evidence," *Anchorage Daily News*, December 11, 2008, 1.

22  Ibid.

23  J. O'Malley, "Scents Put Wade and Schloss in Kincaid Park Area. Hearing: Blood-hounds Tracked the Accused and the Victim, FBI Agents Say," *Anchorage Daily News*, December 10, 2008.

24  J. O'Malley, "Wade's Attorney Tries to Discredit Bloodhounds' Work," *Anchorage Daily News*, August 29, 2008.

25  Ibid.

## NOTES TO HUMAN ODOR AND DOGS' SCENT PERCEPTION

1  W. Neuhaus, "Über die Riechschärfe des Hundes für Fettsäuren," *Zeitschrift für Vergleichende Physiologie* 35 (1953): 527–52.

2  W. Neuhaus, "Die Unterscheidungsfähigkeit des Hundes für Duftgemische," *Zeitschrift für Vergleichende Physiologie* 39 (1956): 25–43.

3  See R. Gerritsen and R. Haak, *K9 Professional Tracking: A Complete Manual for Theory and Training*, (Calgary, Canada: Detselig Enterprises Ltd., 2001), 43.

4  A.I. Spielman, X.N. Zeng, J.J. Leyden, et al. "Proteinacceous Precursors of Human Axillary Odor: Isolation of Two Novel Odor-Binding Proteins," *Experientia* 51 (1995): 40–47.

5  C is a prefix in the metric system denoting a factor of one hundredth ($10^{-2}$).

6  E.A. Eady, M.R. Farmery, J.I. Ross, J.H. Cove, and W.J. Cunliffe, "Effects of Benzoyl Peroxide and Erythromycin Alone and in Combination against Antibiotic-Sensitive and -Resistant Skin Bacteria from Acne Patients," *British Journal of Dermatology* 131, no. 3 (September 1994): 331–336.

7  H.C. Korting, A. Lukacs, and O. Braun-Falco, "Microbial Flora and Odor of the Healthy Human Skin," *Hautarzt* 39, no. 9 (September 1988): 564–568.

8  R.S. Ramatowski, "Composition of Latent Fingerprint Residue," in *Advances in Fingerprint Technology*, ed. H.C. Lee and R.E. Gaensslen (Boca Raton, FL: CRC Press, 2001).

9  M.E. Stewart, M.W. McDonnell, and D.T. Downing, "Possible Genetic Control of the Proportions of Branched-Chain Fatty Acids in Human Sebaceous Wax Esters," *Journal of Investigative Dermatology* 86 (1986): 706–708.

10  Z.T. Halpin, "Individual Odors among Mammals: Origins and Functions," *Advances in the Study of Behavior* 16 (1986): 39–70.

11  E.A. Boyse, "HLA and the Chemical Senses," *Human Immunology*, 15, no. 4 (1986): 391–395.

12  L. Löhner, "Über menschliche Individual- und Regionalgerüche," *European Journal of Physiology* 202, no. 1 (1924): 24–45.

13  D.M. Stoddart, *The Scented Ape: The Biology and Culture of Human Odour* (Cambridge: Cambridge University Press, 1990), 135.

14  R.S. Ramotowski, "Composition of Latent Fingerprint Residue," in *Advances in Fingerprint Technology*, ed. H.C. Lee and R.E. Gaensslen (Boca Raton, FL: CRC Press, 2001), 63–104.

15  S. Silbernagl and A. Despopoulos, *Color Atlas of Physiology*, 6th Edition (New York: Thieme Medical Publications, 2008), 344–361.

16  D. Lancet, "Exclusive Receptors," *Nature* 372 (1994): 321–322.

17  H.W. Wang, C.J. Wysocki, and G.H. Gold, "Induction of Olfactory Receptor Sensitivity in Mice," *Science* 260, no. 5110 (May 14, 1993): 998–1000. And S.L. Youngentob and P.F. Kent, "Enhancement of Odorant-Induced Mucosal Activity Patterns in Rats Trained on an Odorant Identification Task," *Brain Research* 670, no. 1 (1995): 82–88.

## NOTES TO SCENT PROBLEMS AND TRAINING PROBLEMS

1  G.E. Schwartz, I.R. Bell, Z.V. Dikman, M. Fernandez, J.P. Kline, and J.M.Peterson, "EEG Responses to Low-Level Chemicals in Normals and Cacosmics," *Toxicology and Industrial Health* 10, nos. 4–5 (1995): 633–643.

2  N. Sobel, R. Khan, A. Saltman, E. Sullivan, and J. Gabrieli, "The World Smells Different to Each Nostril," *Nature* 402, no. 6757 (1999): 35.

3  J.D. Pierce, X.N. Zeng, E.V. Aronov, G. Preti, and C.J. Wysocki, "Cross-Adaptation of Sweaty-Smelling 3-Methyl-2-Hexonoic Acid by a Structurally Similar, Pleasant Smelling Odorant," *Chemical Senses* 20, no. 4 (1995): 401–411.

4  P. Vroon, *Zonder Geur Geen Emoties* (Amsterdam: De Volkskrant, 1989), 23.

5  R. Gross-Isseroff and D. Lancet, "Concentration Dependent Changes of Perceived Odor Quality," *Chemical Senses* 13, no. 2 (1988): 191–204.

6  D.G. Laing, H. Panhuber, and B.M. Slotnick, "Odor Masking in the Rat," *Physiology & Behavior* 45 (1989): 689–694. See also M. Laska and R. Hudson, "Discriminating

Parts from a Whole: Determinants of Odor Mixture Perception in Squirrel Monkeys, *Saimiri Sciureus*," *Journal of Comparative Physiology A* 173, no. 2 (1993): 249–256.

7 U. Staubli, D. Fraser, R. Faraday, and G. Lynch, "Olfaction and the 'Data' Memory System in Rats," *Behavioral Neuroscience* 101 (1987): 757–765.

8 I. Briewasser, "Fährtenarbeit, die Grenze der Belastbarkeit," *Unsere Hunde* (January 1989): 12.

## NOTE TO PREVENTING INVESTIGATION ERRORS

1 See R. Gerritsen and R. Haak, *K9 Professional Tracking: A Complete Manual for Theory and Training* (Calgary: Detselig Enterprises Ltd., 2001).

# About the Authors

**Ruud Haak** is the author of more than 30 dog books in Dutch and German. Since 1979, he has been the editor-in-chief of the biggest Dutch dog magazine, *Onze Hond (Our Dog)*. He was born in 1947 in Amsterdam, the Netherlands. At the age of 13, he was training police dogs at his uncle's security dog training center, and when he was 15, he worked after school with his patrol dog (which he trained himself) at the Amsterdam harbor. He later started training his dogs in Schutzhund and IPO, and he successfully bred and showed German shepherds and Saint Bernards.

Ruud worked as a social therapist in a government clinic for criminal psychopaths. From his studies in psychology, he became interested in dog behavior and training methods for nose work, especially the tracking dog and the search-and-rescue dog. More recently he has trained drug and explosive detector dogs for the Dutch police and the Royal Dutch Airforce. He is also a visiting lecturer at Dutch, German, and Austrian police dog schools.

In the 1970s, Ruud and his wife, **Dr. Resi Gerritsen**, a psychologist and jurist, attended many courses and symposia with their German shepherds for Schutzhund, tracking dog, and search-and-rescue dog training in Switzerland, Germany, and Austria. In 1979, they started the Dutch Rescue Dog Organization in the Netherlands. With that unit, they attended many operations responding to earthquakes, gas explosions, and lost persons in wooded or wilderness areas. In 1990, Ruud and Resi moved to Austria, where they were asked by the Austrian Red Cross to select and train operational rescue and avalanche dogs. They lived for three years at a height of 6,000 feet (1800 m) in the Alps and worked with their dogs in search missions after avalanches.

With their Austrian colleagues, Ruud and Resi developed a new method for training search-and-rescue dogs. This way of training showed the best results after a major earthquake in Armenia (1988), an earthquake in Japan (1995), two major earthquakes in Turkey (1999), and big earthquakes in Algeria and Iran (2003). Ruud and Resi have also demonstrated the success of their unique training methods for tracking dogs as well as search-and-rescue dogs at the Austrian, Czech, Hungarian, and World Championships, where both were several times the leading champions.

Resi and Ruud have held many symposia and master classes all over the world on their unique training methods, which are featured in their books:

- *K9 Search and Rescue: A Manual for Training the Natural Way*
- *K9 Professional Tracking: A Complete Manual for Theory and Training*
- *K9 Schutzhund: A Manual for IPO Training through Positive Reinforcement*
- *K9 Personal Protection: A Manual for Training Reliable Protection Dogs*
- *K9 Complete Care: A Manual for Physically and Mentally Healthy Working Dogs*
- *K9 Working Breeds: Characteristics and Capabilities*
- *K9 Scent Training: A Manual for Training Your Identification, Tracking, and Detection Dog*

With Simon Prins they wrote: *K9 Behavior Basics: A Manual for Proven Success in Operational Service Dog Training*; and with Dr. Adee Schoon, Ruud wrote *K9 Suspect Discrimination: Training*

**Figure 9.9** Ruud Haak with his German shepherd Yes van Sulieseraad and Malinois Google van het Eldenseveld.

**Figure 9.10** Resi Gerritsen with her Malinois Halusetha's All Power and Malinois Google van het Eldenseveld.

*and Practicing Scent Identification Line-Ups.* All of these books were published by Detselig Enterprises Ltd., Calgary, Canada (now Brush Education Inc.).

Ruud and Resi now live in the Netherlands. They were training directors and international judges for the International Red Cross Federation and the United Nations (OCHA), and they are international judges for the International Rescue Dog Organisation (IRO) and the Fédération Cynologique Internationale (FCI).

At the moment, Ruud and Resi are still successfully training their dogs as detector dogs for search and rescue, drugs, explosives, and IPO Schutzhund. You can contact the authors by e-mail at resigerritsen@gmail.com

# K9 Professional Training Series

**K9 Behavior Basics**
A Manual for Proven Success in Operational Service Dog Training
second edition
Resi Gerritsen • Ruud Haak • Simon Prins
K9 PROFESSIONAL TRAINING SERIES

**K9 Personal Protection**
A Manual for Training Reliable Protection Dogs
second edition
Resi Gerritsen • Ruud Haak
K9 PROFESSIONAL TRAINING SERIES

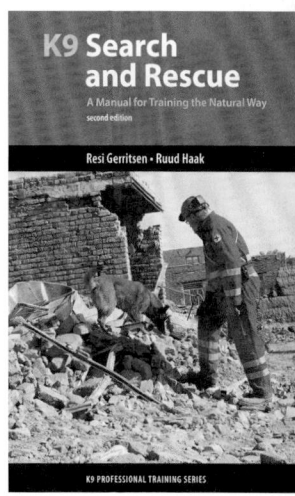

**K9 Search and Rescue**
A Manual for Training the Natural Way
second edition
Resi Gerritsen • Ruud Haak
K9 PROFESSIONAL TRAINING SERIES

**K9 Scent Training**
A Manual for Training Your Identification, Tracking and Detection Dog
Resi Gerritsen • Ruud Haak
K9 PROFESSIONAL TRAINING SERIES

**K9 Schutzhund Training**
A Manual for IPO Training through Positive Reinforcement
second edition
Resi Gerritsen • Ruud Haak
K9 PROFESSIONAL TRAINING SERIES

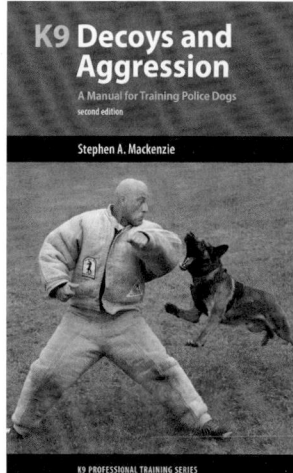

**K9 Decoys and Aggression**
A Manual for Training Police Dogs
second edition
Stephen A. Mackenzie
K9 PROFESSIONAL TRAINING SERIES